Justin Chin: Selected Works

Books by Justin Chin:

Bite Hard
Mongrel: Essays, Diatribes, and Pranks
Harmless Medicine
Burden of Ashes
Attack of the Man-Eating Lotus Blossoms
Gutted
98 Wounds

Justin Chin: Selected Works

Jennifer Joseph
editor

Manic D Press
San Francisco

In Memoriam
Justin Chin
8 September 1969 - 24 December 2015

Thanks to R. Zamora Linmark, Lisa Asagi, the family of Justin Chin, Dave Thomson, Henry Machtay, Kirk Read, Radar Productions. With gratitude to the Manic D authors – past, present, and future – who support our literary endeavors with heart and soul, thank you.

cover photo: Justin Chin reading at *Phantoms of Asia*, 2012, Asian Art Museum of San Francisco. Photograph © Asian Art Museum of San Francisco.

CONTENTS

Despair not, no strange fate befalls
On fearful night in heart, no heroes raised
No monsters vexed, no affliction reached
In dreams of outlaws' tears, this blessed rest

Wave goodbye. The family car pulls down the cul-de-sac and my brother and I wave to Mom. Her silhouette in the tinted back window is a head peeking, sticking out from behind the passenger-seat headrest, a hand waving frantically. Dad waves a bit, but he's driving, hands on the wheel. We wave and wave until the car turns the corner and with a final wave the car is gone and Chepstow Close is laced with a strange silence, as if the car had driven off with all the sounds of the street—children playing, their tricycles crushing the damp leaves piled at the sides of the road, the sound of gates creaking open and closed, the gossiping neighbours, the barking dogs, the Sunday washing of cars, the street football games. I know the neighbours are watching, but we can't see them; they're all indoors, peeking out from behind their dusty curtains. My brother and I shuffle back indoors. The silence that hangs in the street hangs in the house too, as if we had dragged it in on our slippers.

The door flings open and Mom is standing by my bed; she wakes me up and dresses me. She takes me by the hand and walks me to her and my dad's bedroom, and opens the door roughly. Dad is lying in bed, propped up on pillows, watching television. She pushes me forward and orders, "Say goodbye to your father."

"Bye, Dad," I say obediently. I have no idea what is happening. Dad says "Humph," more a grunt than a reply. Quincy, M.E. is about to solve yet another crime. She closes the door and I ask where we're going. Mom says we're going to join my brother at Grandma's and we're not coming back. I panic: What about my stuffed animals? What is to become of them? Who will take care of them? Won't they miss me and get lonely? I had carefully named them all and talked to them every day; they were my best friends. "Bring them along," she says, and we load 12 stuffed toys into the back of a cab. We ride 100 miles, take two ferries, transfer to another cab, ride another 100 miles, cross through the causeway between Singapore and Malaysia in the early dark fluorescent tinge of dawn, and arrive at my grandma's in another country at 6 in the morning. I unload all my stuffed animals but one, the batik tortoise my Aunty Jeck Lan sewed for me as a final project in her home economics class, is missing.

For the next three days, there is a mad buzz around the house. Mom eventually calls Dad and he comes to pick her up, but by then I have already been enrolled in a new school and on Sunday afternoon Mom and Dad drive away, leaving me with my guardians, my cousins, my brother, and Rupert the Bear, Yong-Yong, Humpty, Big Dog, Kola Pola Nice Bear, PiPi Xiong Mao, Winnie, Yellow Shirt, Big Monster, A-Po, and Nice Face. The adults assure me that the one lost turtle—I hadn't even named him—is a small loss. After all, look at what I still have, they say.

I wasn't supposed to be here so soon. The argument between my parents pushed the timetable of my life ahead two and a half years—only then was I supposed to be sent 200 miles to Singapore to go to school. When he's a bit older, the adults would say, plotting my future, envisioning my brilliant future with the advantages of the superior educational system across the border. But now, in mid-semester, in my first year of schooling, I am in the small house my mother grew up in. She grew up in different houses, but it is here where I imagine her in all the stories that she tells me. This is what I see in the house: My mother is teasing her hair into a beehive. Aqua Net in one hand spraying, hairbrush in the other working a combination pat-comb-lift. We are somewhere in the '60s. Crackling black-and-white TV sets beam Americana in static-lined pictures across living rooms across the state, mixed in with local programming favourites. Elvis, in all his Pelvis and lip-curl glory, is in her head, she's part-singing, part-humming "Love Me Tender" with the wrong lyrics, looking like one of the Vandellas, who wants to look like a Supreme, but Chinese. Elvis in her head because my grandfather burst into her room and grabbed the record off the player and tossed it out the window. "What's this Devil's music? It's not singing. It's shouting," he yells, before snatching the record player so he can relax in the living room reading his newspaper while Jim Reeves soothes with "My Hand in the Lord's."

If he were to look in the room now, he'd see her plotting with her brothers on how to convince him to allow her to go to nursing school. He ripped the first application to shreds and tossed it out of the same window Elvis went through two days ago. Nursing and Elvis, both wingless creatures flung to the ground. "Good daughters from good families become teachers." A broken record repeated out of the old man. "A nurse...what would people say?" he harrumphs, and seeks solace in Burl Ives crooning "What a Friend We Have in Jesus."

The first few years were the hardest. My guardians—my grandmother and my aunt Jessie—were already taking care of my cousins Karen and

Sharon, whose father had died and whose mother, we were eventually told, had abandoned them when they were young.

We were like some motley bunch of orphans; and I always enjoyed fairy tales about children who were orphans and had cruel stepparents. These stories ended with the children blissfully happy and the cruel stepparents reformed or dead; the children either discovered that their real parents were actually alive and under some sorceress's spell, or were adopted into loving homes with pets.

To help ease my missing my mom and dad, I was given a small framed photo of them, taken by my dad's brother some years earlier in the cable cars on the way to Sentosa Island. I was in the cable car too, but in the photo all you can see is the top of my head, just a small crown of hair. For the first few weeks I clutched the photo and cried myself to sleep. I put the photo beside my pillow. Sometimes I could hear my brother, who slept in the upper bunk bed, sniffling tears too. He had a photo of the family at a holiday to Genting Highlands a few years back.

Going to Singapore used to be fun; it was a family vacation, with shopping trips to Yaohan and the Japanese bookstore in Plaza Singapura, maybe even a few dollars to spend in the amusement arcades there. But this was different. This was a different trip altogether. This time I was left here for some reason I did not fully comprehend just yet. I hadn't even grasped the concept of time: What was a week? A month? A semester?

My parents visited for a weekend every month. In the first year of their visits, the drive took more than six hours. They had to cross one river where there was no bridge. Instead, there was a rickety wooden ferry that brought the cars back and forth. Often, there was a long line of cars backed up. Previously, many years ago, to make that trip from my little hometown to the big city there would be five such rivers to cross, but the city councils and the state governments started building concrete bridges that linked them, and the ferrymen and the food vendors that lived off the maddening rivers all disappeared and went to other pastures. But this one bridge never got made; perhaps the river was too deep, or too wide. The ferry portion of the journey was the most dreaded part of the journey. After the long wait, there was always the fear that the ferry would capsize. If we were en route home for the holidays, my mother would always turn to the back seat and tell us to *pray for safety*. Other times, we waited at Chepstow Close for our parents to show up at the gate in the evening, having said our prayers for their safety.

In my childlike mind, my parents' death was the most horrific thing I could ever imagine, more than Springy the Pekinese dying, more than losing my cherished stuffed bears. Once, while waiting for my mom at the hair salon, I watched her being placed under the huge heated-air dome that crowned her curler-pinned new 'do like some science-fiction contraption. "What's that? What are they doing?" I asked, and Mom looked up from her *Women's Weekly* magazine and said, "Oh, they're cooking me. Soon I'll be dead." I shrieked and started crying horribly, but everyone in the salon laughed and thought how cute it all was that I was so afraid of the hairdryer going on my mom. And now I imagined my parents in the car, sinking in the depths of the muddy river, and I was fearful, thinking of all my childish sins that God could punish me for by drowning my parents, until I saw the blue Mercedes Benz chug up the cul-de-sac.

Eventually, of course, the bridge got built, and the drive time was significantly shortened, if not the worry: There were stories of timber lorries smashing into cars and crushing them like tin cans, cement mixers being hauled on flatbed trucks that fell off and crushed cars, cars that smashed into water buffaloes, killing all the passengers while the buffalo walked off unscathed, all sorts of horrible twisted wrecks of car accidents. The prayers for safety changed, the worries continued.

Now the ferries were no more; bank to bank, all the rivers and channels were connected. Even the Penang ferry, the historic mass of timber and steel that fueled local novelists' and filmmakers' imaginations, which for years ferried thousands of countrymen from the mainland to the island, was threatened by the majestic Penang bridge. We were told it was a long suspension bridge, just like the legendary Golden Gate Bridge. We were told wrong; it was a regular bridge, with columns plunging firmly into the unseen bed of the channel. Only the heavy toll on the bridge kept the ferries going for a few more months.

I was endlessly fascinated by bridges. It was the year-end Primary Two examinations—fail this and you're left behind for a whole year. We were given a list of 50 words to learn, of which 25 would he chosen for the spelling and dictation finals. The examination was to be carried out over the school's public address system. That way, the entire grade of 13 classes could do the examination at the same time. Instead of the naked word, the examination sheet distributed to us came in the form of sentences with an appropriate blank, and we were to fill in the blank as prompted by the voice on the loudspeaker. *Number 6. Potato. John's mother is peeling a potato, poe-tay-toe, potato in the kitchen.* It all seemed quite simple, really, and being the annoying overprepared child that I was, I managed to fill in all the blanks before the prompt. *Number 7. Magazine. Mary is reading a magazine, ma-gah-zine, magazine in her room.* Since I finished the examination early, I decided to pass the time by constructing a bridge from my desk to the neighbouring desk using my two rulers. I carefully tucked the end of one ruler under my boxy pencilcase as a foundation and stuck the other ruler tinder my neighbour's pencilcase. There was a small gap between the two so I stole the ruler from the boy behind me to close the gap. By this time, of course, the proctor had come to my desk and was red in the face, screaming "What do you think you're doing?!" I looked at him blankly. This was before I had any conception of what examinations really were. (That I would discover the following year, when half of the class ended up in tears and anguished weeping when they could not finish their mock listening comprehension exams.) The proctor brought his hand down in a karate chop right in the middle of my bridge, looking not unlike some space monster destroying a Tokyo bridge in *Ultraman.* If you're finished, if you think you're so smart, just sit there until everyone else is finished and don't disturb anyone." I spent the rest of the hour making a little bridge with my ruler, bridging pencil case to pencil case, pushing my eraser across their precarious bounce, though the Stadler eraser my aunt had swiped from her office desk was far too fat and it often careened off the ruler bridge, plunging into the depths of my desk—my own instant miniature river disaster. I imagined who would be in that eraser car: that fat fairy Winston Lee who sat at the front of the class, who insisted on being called Winnie and answering every question the teacher asked; or that evil girl from the Convent of the Holy Infant Jesus who sat at the back of the bus and terrorized us. The best scenario had them both as best friends on their way to extra math tuition when that horrible horrible accident happened.

I am a bad driver. I have no depth perception and cannot gauge distances very well. I am very bad at parking, though I am improving. My dad is a good driver. Lying on the backseat of the car, I watched the speedometer and the blinking lights in the dashboard reflected on the windows as he drove us home. Even through the worst rainstorms and the heaviest traffic, we knew we would be safe. Even as he overtook timber lorries and tankers filled with explosive gases. When we went to visit my paternal grandparents in Sungei Lembing, their little tin-mining hometown 50 miles away, my dad would drive us back after dinner. In the twisty winding roads, where one false turn could send the car crashing into 60-foot ravines of mud and tin mining sludge, I slumped against the car door, listening to the tunes blaring from the car stereo: Lipps Inc.'s "Funkytown" and Donna Summer belting "Hot Stuff" and "Bad Girl"—how my brother and I laughed ourselves silly every time the disco whistles blew staccato beats on that album, it was the queerest thing we had ever heard! Both cassettes recommended by the salesgirl at Pahang Supermarket: "Good for driving, very fast music, very good," she assured. Even as the night fell, and insects flew bugspeed into the windshield and the fog rolled in, and the car reverberated with cowbells, whistles, tambourines, and synthesized disco beats, I knew I was safe.

Once, on the way back from a family vacation in Genting Highlands Resort, the brakes failed on the steep descent from the mountains and we went flying down the narrow mountain roads at breakneck speed, but Dad, in his calm fatherly way, brought the car to a noisy stop in the stench of smoking tires and screeching hand-brakes.

This was how fathers drove. In all weathers and conditions, in all adversity and through rising floodwaters, all to bring the family home safe.

Every year, we judge the severity of a monsoon by the bridges, which ones are covered, flooded over, which ones are washed out, and which are still accessible. The phone would ring and a relative would be calling to report that a certain road or a certain bridge was washed out, under X number of feet of water, and would tell us which other bridges were inaccessible and which ones were wholly swept away, leaving a gashing chasm in the road, a death trap for unsuspecting cars to fall into its torrential maw.

In spite of the worry about floods, I loved the monsoon. I thought it was beautiful how the rain beat down in the heaviest downpour for days, crashing on the awning outside my bedroom window. I loved the deafening sound of the heavy drops smashing against the tin awning, creating such a percussive racket no one could hear anyone talk. I loved the fearsome crack of thunder and lightning and how the flash of electric in the sky could light up the whole dark night so supremely.

We looked to see how much water was rushing in the drains around the house and around the housing estate to gauge how full the storm drains were and whether the river was at a high tide, which promised a flooding for sure, or at the reprieve of low tide. By this time, the gardens around the estate were all waterlogged, prized flowerbeds ruined, blades of grass sticking out like paddy. House dogs searched for any dry spot to curl and sleep.

In the house, the marker of whether to worry about flooding was the drainage hole in the kitchen floor. If water started to come out of the hole, the situation looked grim. The water level in the toilet bowls would rise.

Then bricks were brought in, the refrigerator and washing machine had to be lifted and the bricks placed under them to raise them above any flood line. The gas tanks on the stove were disconnected and put on the tables. Dinner would be Heinz baked beans on white bread, or sardine sandwiches. The lower cabinets in the kitchen were emptied, and then we'd wait. Most times, the rain eased up and the waters subsided, but on a few occasions we actually flooded.

My first flood was in kindergarten days. Furniture was moved, and we stayed on the second level of the house. It was very Swiss Family Robinson, I thought. Fishes, shoals of gray guppies, not the sort you'd want to catch and keep, not when you could get the beautiful multicoloured ones at the fish shop for a dollar, and a small catfish, whiskers and all, swam into the dining room. Always after the floods there was a massive clean-up. Mud and sludge from the drains, swamps, and rivers stained unmercifully, and the inches-thick layer was a challenge to scrape off and wash out.

Even as we were waiting for the floodwaters to subside, Mom reassured us that it wouldn't be so bad, that it was all right—after all, she reminded us, God had made a covenant with Noah that he would never kill the world by flooding anymore; the next time, it would be fire.

But it's not always monsoon. Sometimes it's so hot and dry that the tarmac steams and you see mirages, shimmering pools of water, little oases in the middle of the road.

We drive on the road leading under the new bridge to view the changing, unfamiliar river, the same one that has been meandering there all our lives. Now you can see the kampongs and ramshackle shacks, the poor fisher-folk, the stuff picturesque tourist postcards are made of; but postcards don't show the pollution, the poverty, and the scabby children playing in the diesel sludge of the river. *Wish You Were Here.*

We stop under the bridge and get out to look. My dad says that somewhere he owns a small fishing sampan; Mom says it's probably sunken already.

We look back at our small town, not so small anymore. Across the way, a dilapidated ferry is slowly making its way across the river; a lone man and his companion are sitting in the sputtering grumble of its engine, grinding its way across the fluid expanse where once, many years ago, on a bridge, upstream, I fished for stingrays that lurked on the murky floor where the salty ocean clashes with the calm city mud.

Tied

This is a tin-mining town with just one traffic
light at the town square and floods
every December, guaranteed,
and you're just another one
of the women in this town
who raises her kids, takes care
of the house and helps her husband at the shop.
You don't know better
when your husband brings home
the town seamstress as his second wife,
She gives birth to two kids.
You raise them as your own
and they know it too.
They call you Ma & Ah-Ma,
and they call her Mother.
What reason has she got to be jealous of you?
What does she know about childbirth?
You've done it thirteen times,
watched four of them die.
Your friends have all left
since the bottom fell out
of tin, years ago. They've moved
to the big town now. Your children
have all grown and moved too.
Now, you're tied down to your husband
since his stroke. What do you know
about business? About running
a pig farm? You let the second wife
take over the business.
She tells the old man you slander
her, poison her children's minds
against her. What can you do?
The old man takes her side.
What does she know about
taking care of the old man?
All day, you're cooking his favorite
dishes for him, feeding him, washing him, amusing him.

Your children tell you to leave.
Sell the house and bring the old man
to town where he can stay with them.
But he won't let you. He wants to live here,
in this tin-mining town where
everything shuts down, closes up
at 5:30 p.m. What do you know
about leaving? Where have you ever gone?
You hide the money your children give you.
You know the second wife takes the money
the children give to the old man.
She'll take yours too, if she could.
She tells him she will send it back
to the village for him.
You know the old man doesn't trust anyone with his money.
He knows his second wife steals his money.
He starts keeping his money in his shirt pocket.
The first time you have money of your own.
What do you do with your money?
You spend it during Chinese New Year,
and for your grandchildren's birthdays.
You buy a new color TV for the house.
You lie and say your children bought it
for you. Now, the old man watches the news
and anything that's on TV. Now, you have time
to make quick trips to the neighbors'.
You know that is not enough.
You want to play cards with your friends,
spend your evenings watching those never-ending Cantonese serials,
visit your children in different towns,
live in different states,
wash the pork smell and the smell
of the old man's vomit off your hands,
but you can't, you're still tied down, here,
in this tin-mining town with one traffic light
and annual floods. In December,
you have your chickens, raised from eggs,
and your cat to worry about.

A History of Geography

America is a place far away,
as far as London/ Australia/ or Canada
any Western country where people speak English,
All a page in an atlas/ a place on a map, can't drive/ walk/
    take a bus to —
I want to go there, so I buy magazines, take a Biro felt pen,
    draw arrows to people in the photographs & write my name
    on their foreheads,
I want to go there so I fuck their people,
don't care if they're good-looking/ or turn me on or not,
I let them take me,
do what they want with me
even if it hurts me bad/ makes me bleed/ makes me bruise/ sore/ & angry/
sad/ satisfied/ & happy/ mad/ desolate,
let them do what they want with a slab of meat
because they're giving me a place I cannot get to.
So I throw my legs up in the air,
spread them in toilets/ spread them in parks/ spread them in
    hotel rooms,
rich hotels/ with real fancy sheets and bedspreads/ with mint
    chocolates and strawberries by starched white pillows &
    fancy room service/ & nice uniformed bellmen/ &
    receptionists who look at me and know what I'm doing/ cos
    they want to do it too/ done it before,
maybe cheap rundown hotels/ with shared bathrooms & thin
    walls/ creaky beds/ bed lice & stinking men.
But I don't care cos I'm in America/ in London/ in Australia/
    in France/ in anywhere but this town.
This town where I am the son of a generation/ lost
to 25 years of what price paradise.
This town so clean and green, everything wiped over with
    Dettol every week,
wiped so clean, they take away your insides
& give you dog biscuits & standard rations to replace what
they've disinfected.

I hold things I cannot say in my mouth,
I hold acts I cannot do in my chest,
hold a bitter stinking love in my groin.
Let them wipe away everything else,
wipe me/ disinfect me/ hose me down,
but I got what nobody else got
and they can't wipe that away
not even with their industrial strength bleach.
& I don't/won't care what they make me sing/chant justice,
     equality, peace, progress, prosperity, happiness for my
     life,
it's all words that I sing/ chant/ move my lips/
know what it means,
and that is dangerous.
Wrap myself in newsprint,
wrap myself in satellite transmissions,
wrap myself in truth/ lies/ truth/ half truths,
believe what I wrap myself in knowing
I cannot go back.

They want to distill me,
take the queer sky out of my body.
Let it sit, simmer until my fire burns up in itself.
& when I am dark/ when I have no more light/ when I am no
     more an abomination/ when I am no more shame/ when I am face
     again/ when the collective being of me worships god, family,
     education and the collective administrative silver spoon,
then I will be back in the fold.
The prodigal child, back from exile.

Please let me live
and rage in the realm of wonderment,
to know that the hand in the glove is not the fascist halal
     rationed kiss that makes me feel like a stranger/ an
     outsider in my own.
Let me live in all that my blood is mine,
in the color of spirits
backwards.

I am blind,
      born blind, spirits come to me in polaroids of abstract
      paintings that throw mud and saliva on my eyes to see
      the new issue of *Blue Boy*,
who show me that love is deaf,
      born deaf, spirits come to me as a bluesy lullaby, a
      cat's howl at night that fills my ears/ that I can't
      hear/ don't want to hear/ whispers yes that chokes me
till I can't speak, born dumb,
spirit is a voice that no one will hear because everybody is
      born deaf, dumb and blind
in the bright lights holding us in a circle jerk, to the
      music we speak of nothing that cannot find our minds.
& I am in this world of pirates, prayers, ascensions, coups,
      attacks, counterattacks, shadows, illness, deceptions,
      manipulations, addictions, metaphysicians, hyperboles,
      poetics, politics, plays, perspiration and love.

This Is Your Life

Not much, is it?
After dumping cement
on the bits of lawn she can't reach
with her old lawnmower, she goes
to her sons' room, sits on the edge
of their bed with tears in her eyes,
points to Jesus on the wall.
>   *Pray. When you're scared*
>   *of the dark, just look at him.*
She kisses them goodnight
and makes sure they have their socks on.
Five months later, the picture of Jesus is gone.
She discovers that it violated
"thou shall not worship any graven image"
it's sinful and the picture disappears one day.

This is her life.
She paints the doors and cupboards black
so the dirt won't show.
But dust is white and that
still shows.

Now, she sips iced tea and wonders
why her sons are so distant.
One who is so scared of himself that he crumbles
like an almond cookie.
The other who loves his fag-self so much, it hurts
her. *Pray, walk close to the lord.*

She remembers them growing up
differently. Now, she realizes
why one could never speak to her,
why he always turned silent when she spoke
of *God's punishment to sinners.*
She tells them of all the sacrifices
she made for them, how
they must make her proud and how much they do

make her proud. Is it not so much to ask for?
It is late now, this is her
life and the stuffed bears collecting dust
and sunlight, the empty beds,
the same vague letters and the old
photographs can't hold her in place.
Clinging to her bible and daily devotions, prayers
and church work, this is her life.
Ask her how she's living it.

Flying the Red Eye

Flying the red eye with bodies breathing heavy all around me
     silent as cows strapped into corrals fed cleaned and fed
     again.
25G beside me has his tray table propped on his belly and is
     snoring but doesn't hear himself because his headset is
     loud on channel five.
He tells me that he travelled first class last year once
     because his sister's friend had connections and it was
     great champagne steak fresh fruit the works he says
     offering me his dinner roll *Jesus Christ this is hard as*
     stools ya want it.
The toilet is the only escape from the smoking section but
     there's pee everywhere it's hard to piss in turbulence and
     I miss too and I tell myself it's only six more hours.
Can't see any good clouds on the red eye and the stars are
     not out tonight or maybe they're there but I can't see
     them you see stars in first class I'm told but it's all
     darkness outside.
Airports are like bookends and planes they scare me big
     chunks of synchronized metal and plastic snatching people
     away from the earth.
The best kinds of airports are those where you don't have to
     walk where conveyor belts drag you to where you want to go
     because there's nothing worse than having to walk miles to
     throw someone on a plane then walk again to get them back.
I sit with the ferns with my carry-on luggage and wave
     goodbye to 25G beside me his sister is really quite sweet.
Cars pull up and people are flying into each other's arms and
     lips and little children bouncing in the backseat trying to
     grab daddy's baseball cap and dogs licking car windows and
     trunks opening and closing and french kissing and I am
     going home.

Smell

My grandmother loads the washing machine.
    I overhear her ask
                  my mother why my clothes

smell *so funny.*

    It is the smell of raw lamb's meat.

My brother's clothes had
                a similar smell
when he came back from England, she said.

It is the smell of the West.

One day at home, I came through the door
and found my grandmother sitting on the sofa
in front of the television crying.
"What happened?" I asked. I was concerned.

She had, all afternoon, been watching
a Discovery channel documentary:
the migration of the wildebeests.

The wildebeesties in their annual migration
had to splash their way across a crocodile infested river,
many were savagely snacked on by the crocs
who lurked waiting, disguised as floating debris with peepers.

This upset her gravely.
"Why doesn't the government build a bridge for them?" she asks me.

At my grandmother's wake, my father was asked
to say a few words. He was a surprise.
My dad, he, the archetypical stoic Chinese father,
in so few mumbly words, in such a simple direct way,
was all at once genuine and heartfelt, funny and sorrowful.

He had insisted on wearing his tan golf shorts
to the funeral, until my mother intervened and
a pair of dark gray trousers was dug out of my suitcase,
hemmed with safety pins and duct tape.

He was saved from being the most inappropriately dressed
by my cousin who works for MTV Asia, and who showed up
in a midriff-baring outfit. Her mother later apologizes for her.
"Her clothes all don't have the middle part," she tells us.

What the '80s Meant to Me

The '80s were much bigger than its popular culture, bigger than pop music and happythings. There was so much more happening, the world was changing, decisions were being made that were going to affect how I and my friends and family were going to live. But what did my tender hinges know of all that? And so like mallrats walking deafly, hypnotized by the Muzak, I walked right into the trap of leisure, the opiate of my senses and my heart. I traded my pickled brains for consumer choice, became the grateful lab rat of The Grand Plan that was gunning toward the greater social blah.

I don't know at what point it happened. It was as if I was waking from a dream of naïve intentions. I opened my eyes and I saw that things could never be the same.

You grow into your heart and your understanding of its past. And you wonder where it has been all this time.

This time period is more than the wink of nostalgia or the serious dash of memory. Of course, I have been selective; I have weeded and pruned and clung to the good bits. I've edited the timeline, crumpled the chronology, merged events, left many things out, exaggerated, lied; I've made things up and I saw things I never saw. I have not told the full story, or a true one. There is no full or true.

I used to believe that a story was only as good as its intentions. And what do intentions count for in these so little days. Give me my sense of romance. Give me my revisionism. Give me my nostalgia.

Everything of my queer life, I discovered when things were still mine to hold. Everything discovered, when innocence meant not knowing regret; it was a hot fuck, and AIDS, which showed up so late in that part of the world, was something that was still a rumor. Freddie Mercury was still alive. Rock Hudson had just kissed Linda Evans. The full brunt of the heartlessness was waiting around the corner like the most patient mugger.

These days, I see people I used to hang out with, skip school with; the ones who aren't dead or burnt out, are working their little dead-end jobs, living for the weekend so they can get leglessly spun. People I used to see at ACT UP and Queer Nation meetings, the ones who aren't dead, are working at the designer outlet store, having their little software jobs, clawing onto boards of directors, running for political office, positions we once scorned.

We've all grown up so fast, though no faster than any other thing in the world.

My mother always said to me, "Enjoy your youth, you're only young once, you'll never have it again. One day, you'll find that you're too old for so many things. Now stop wasting your time and go study."

I used to know so much, and then I grew up.
I used to believe, and then I grew up.
I used to hope, and then I grew up.
I used to be so beautiful and angry, and then I knew better.

Bitter

Bitterness comes as revolution,
cyclic, a snake
biting its tail scales,
a dog nipping its tail hairs, bitter,
continuity achieved by subtlety,
perceptions played out,
questions followed by answers,
ask, answer, some days
you will know, others
you wake to nothing of the same,
the smell of washed grass,
I have this theory: the rain
each drop, big as bees, falls
with a velocity to bore into the ground,
tilling the grass smell out
of the air pockets in the earth,
the pine cones and the sea smell
saltiness washed clean with Absolut,
this is another country,
this is a different place,
the water tastes different
and the Indian money changer
with the stained dhoti and turban
smelling of coconut oils and incense,
sitting cross-legged at his pavement box store
respects you for your money,
and your whiteness stands out
like wine stains on the hotel sheets,
where I spilled a half bottle
as we wrestled, our naked bodies
pressed against the sweaty halfjest,
facing the expansiveness
of the night and the buzzing
traffic, plays
its points of red and yellow
against the window panes
while we lay watching the stars

quiver and descend to inches
before our eyes as strangers
start to sprout hair all over
their arms, faces, legs and slowly
turn into large orangutans driving taxicabs,
and the universe churns around us
like a ride at Disneyland,
disappearing into flat
unbroken scheme.
These were the lost years,
writing really bad poems,
arguing with border guards,
this Walkman is not new,
there's no tax anyway,
reading incomprehensible Beckett plays,
discussing Gide and Orton
tripping on dope bought from the bellboy,
cheap wine from the Japanese departmental store,
working on my tan,
trying to add inches to my arms,
listening to you detail your research
on crossculturalisms, here,
as we get off at the station
built to look like a mosque
with the grandeur of bright mosaic
tiles spiraling up dome structures
and intricately craved wood
panelings to hide the grime
and the weary travelers,
rudely shouting at everybody.
In the restroom, I squat
hovering over the hole in the floor
trying to work the uneasiness
out of my stomach as I hear scraping
of feet in the stall beside me,
under the partition, there are two pairs
of shoes, moving in a slow, frantic,
desperate dance, trying to carve
a small slice of validity, to find their heaven

in this hemisphere of spent contradictions,
in this two feet of shit-odored
space, they have found their judgment
and I leave them
to find a pay phone,
my father tells me that the sultana is dead,
the TV programmings have been replaced
with Koranic dirges and everybody
is expected to wear black armbands:
mandatory mourning will be checked on
by the police, so he wears an armband even
while playing all eighteen holes of golf,
to be Chinese here is a *bloody crime*,
he says and tells me to come home soon.
Clutching our tickets to the crosswise
third-class seats, we slouch backwards
towards the darkness, feeling
the close and warmth of our bodies
disentangle and the distance, marked
by the ashes of burning cane fields sticking
to our flesh, the attraction between two bodies
defined beyond gravity
grows heavy as the night falls,
and waving kampung children
accompanied by their elders and parents
give way to paddy fields and tobacco plantations,
lit by night lights and the glow
of the owner's small huts,
speed in front of our field of vision
hushing us to sleep, until
the feeling of urgency wakes me,
heart beating like slacks in a bicycle chain,
I find your body twitching ecstatically
while you rub yourself and metal shards
trickle out of your pants zipper
and turn rusty as I catch them
in my palm before they hit the floor,
the red dust etches itself into the
lines of my hands and the Nonya woman

sitting across the aisle, facing me,
takes my hands, spits into them,
the metal cuts into my hands
and I am left holding the remnants
of our sex, like an offering
to saints unknown, gods unbelieved,
searching for the spiritual
in the physicalness of your body,
dust weaves a maze into our bones,
femur holding suspended fragments
of torn secrecy, jealousy, bitter,
hip bone framing the ravishing, all
held in place with ligaments
fragile as pins and cobwebs,
straining to the lure of hunger,
as we make our way in the splash
of early morning sunlight, yellow
throwing long drawn out shadows
on the walls, through the first-class carriage,
through the recycled air-conditioned air,
smelling of sweating passengers, bleary-eyed
agog at the English-dubbed, the original
Cantonese captioned, kung fu movie
on the small TV screen, dangling
like bait from the ceiling,
to the dining car where
the overpriced cheese sandwiches melt
deliciously sticky and rancid.
The pull of the station brings us
to our destination,
as we set on the platform,
a swarm of brown-skinned boys, all
flashing their brightest Colgate smiles
want to take your backpack, help you
find a hotel, take you to lunch,
let you take them to dinner;
I am not an entity here,
I am competition in their minds,
more likely some cheap slut, a paid whore

who can be bested easily, they know that.
We find our regular boarding house
and the German expatriate,
a longtime resident, greets us and displays
the new boy he picked up in the park,
gave a good scrubbing to and dressed
in neatly pressed schoolboy outfits
for as long as the skinny wide-eyed
fawning boy wants to give handjobs.
The boy offers to do your laundry,
the English woman, a new resident,
invites us for a drink up on the roof
this evening, everybody seems glad
to see you again and the voices
flood into us like madness, pulling
us into the tenderness of untruth.
I invent space, poison, bitter,
snake bites, safety,
fester, if you boil roses
for twenty hours with a teaspoon
of fine sugar, stirring
clockwise, then steaming your face
in the saccharin fumes,
you will be loved, I invent
sweeping, mementos, maturity
and still, nothing
moves, stillness holds your tongue
and it breaks into thorns
sharp enough to pierce through
penitent flesh, wrapping itself
like a python squeezing the last
out of what's left of the moon
reflected on the river as the peddlers
calmly row their sampans laden
with tourist trinkets and vegetables
home; I know the temples
of gold and saffron
that burn incense and powders
on the tongue, deviled,

cutting sinners to jewels
washed in front of Buddhas
with smooth nipples and Egyptian eyes
that said *stay*
and you did.
Lying in the room, cast
a strange orange by the cellophane paper
over the windows, we laid plans,
mapping the fluidity of your life
and mine: I will go south,
to the East Coast to the sea, home
eventually, you will stay and try find
another boy: stranger angels
have beset us, and trains
are stories of sacraments
melting on the tongue, holy,
unspoken, blessed, and thoroughly
immaterial, totally bloodless,
the middleman calls,
there is no hardness
left, your body,
opaque, dense as familiarity,
leaves no stains, no inventions;
the German has found a new boy,
the train is delayed:
an elephant caused a derailment,
the platform is wheels, nothing
can hurt, I float in sea foam,
fine rain and bitter salt,
disenchanted, drawn to decency, shaping
pictures to memory that redefine
visions, transforming virginities,
pure, burning
in the smell of cloves and lines
etched into your palm, kissed
with no exhilarating lips, yes,
it will be a suffering,
this is the tao of the situation, bitterness,
balance achieved by the necessity

of lies, all these lingual guilts,
cruel, bitter, bite hard
this morning, by the window watching
the monsoon splatter itself against the panes,
I watched the neighbor children
splashing in the puddles, holding
plastic bags hoping to catch tadpoles
that will later turn to great
brown toads with lumps and peeling skins,
some days you get all the answers
and bitterness is a root, incriminating
and valuable, it approaches,
with glinting hooks swinging uncertainty,
linking the measure of evenness
and the weight of healing, all
hurling towards impotence, possessed,
barriers to superstitions, bitter, free
and for all to see.

Sold

One toot means lunch, two toots means quitting time.
You'll get the hang of it.
Just take this knob thing here, screw it to this flap-
thing here,
and put the whole thing in this tray, here.
You'll get the hang of it.
Do it today, tomorrow, week after, next year, and
you can do it blindfolded with one arm one leg while
chewing gum and whistling Dixie.
All at the same time.
Here have some. Do you chew gum?
Passes the time you know.
Me I chew gum and imagine the boyfriend's hand up my thigh.
You got a boyfriend? Should see mine.
You'll want his hand up your thigh too.
Gee, I love your hair. What do you do with it?
Mine's hopeless. A head of pubic hair.
What conditioner do you use?
Gum sorta stops you from going on the munchies.
See Row-6-#-3-Mathilda there?
Two years ago she looked like Zsa Zsa Gabor young.
Acted like she was too.
Now pig-woman. Gum passes the time you know.
Here have some. Do you chew gum? You got a boyfriend?
I love your hair? What conditioner do you use?
Do you like movies? A bunch of us go to the movies Thursday.
Or maybe go bowling. But mostly we go movies with happy endings.
We like love stories. We like to have a good cry.
Do you like movies? Do you like gum?
Do you want your boyfriend's hand up your thigh?
Do you have a boyfriend?
You'll get the hang of it.
Put the whole thing in this cart here. Passes the time.
What do you do with it? One toot lunch.
Zsa Zsa Gabor at Row-6-#-3. Pig-woman with 6 kids. Do you chew gum?
Today, tomorrow, week after you'll get the hang of it.
One long toot means fire drill. If you're lucky.

We get to go to the courtyard and gossip.
Two toots quit one long toot gossip one toot lunch.
You'll get the hang of it. I love your hair.
Do you like movies? Maybe bowling with a good cry?
What gum you use? Here have some.
Put the whole pig-woman in this cart, here.
I love your movies with a good cry and happy endings.
Munchies stops you going tomorrow. Lunch toot.
Boyfriend toot. Movie toot. Bowling toot. Happy endings toot.
Pig-woman toot. Gum chewing toot. Fire toot.
Flap-thing-knob-thing toot.
You'll get the hang of it.

May, 1988. University of Hawai'i, Manoa campus. To be exact: a classroom on the fourth floor of the dilapidated Kuykendall Building where the English department and classes are held. Faye Kicknosway, poet and professor in Creative Writing, is wrapping up the Spring semester with her annual "Folder Poets", a reading series showcasing students from her advanced poetry writing workshop. The star of the class is Lois-Ann Yamanaka who's writing these mind-blowing poems in Pidgin, the island vernacular.

An hour before the event, we do a quick run-through. Two students who are not in our class enter the room. Faye introduces them to us as budding poets from her beginning creative writing class. They, too, will be reading their poems (as if we aren't intimidated enough by Lois-Ann). Of the two, the skinny guy with the buzz cut, black-framed glasses, and British accent is the one I will forever remember.

His name is Justin, and Faye, bless her heart, has slated him to read after Lois-Ann. The two are sandwiched in the middle—centerpieces bookended by Bukowski, Ginsberg, and Plath third-rate wannabes—which explains why the event does not gain momentum until Lois-Ann takes over the mic and transforms into the in-your-face teenager Tita, who has everyone belly-aching from laughing as she reminds everyone that the most memorable parts about growing up are also the most painful and hilarious.

Then Faye calls on Justin who, head down, walks to the front of the room with a piece of paper. "Sold," he announces. "One toot means lunch, two toots means quitting time," he begins, then, looking at us, adds: "You'll get the hang of it," as if reassuring us that nothing in life is ever too difficult to manage, fathom, overcome. Before we know it, the shy Journalism major, who is most likely the youngest poet in the room, is performing a stand-alone dialogue, in the persona of a gossip-driven woman. Line after line, we watch him, a fierce word warrior, wow us with his wit and playful language, verve and brazenness.

"You got a boyfriend?" he asks, as if we are part of the poem (because, by this time, it feels like we are). "Should see mine," he brags, "you'll want his hand up your thigh too." Then, as if the punch line is not enough, he delivers another blow: "Gee, I love your hair. What do you do with it? / Mine's hopeless. A head of pubic hair."

We bust out laughing—from shock from surprise from awe from everything that poetry is supposed to do when a poet takes Frank O'Hara's advice and just "go on your nerve." And "Sold" is fierceness amplified. Heavy on humor, frankness, wit, with references to pop culture, it offers us a preview of the uncompromising and unabashed artist.

After the reading, we flock around Justin, reintroduce ourselves and congratulate him for blowing us away, for showing us what Faye has been trying to tell us all semester long: Don't hold back or your poems won't shine. On the drive back to my dorm, all Lois and I do is talk about Justin and how exciting and interesting our class would be if we had his talent, his edge, his energy in our workshop. A wish that, a semester later, will come true, thanks to our teacher Faye, who suggests we form a writing group, along with two other writers—Lisa Asagi and Lori Takayesu.

Thus is how the history of our friendship and shared desire to be writers begins.

Back When I Knew Who I Was

i was content to spend my afternoons
wondering what co-dependant meant
not realizing that those lazy
humid daylight hours was better
spent figuring out the physics
of dependency and codeine dreams

back when i knew who i was
i was much better than i ever thought i was
i could conjugate fuck like nobody's business
    fuck me, fuck you, fuck it, fuck him, fuck her
    fuck them, fuck yourself, holy fuck, goddamnfuckit
i could shovel dead pets off the driveway
    that my aunt ran over on her way to choir practice
    and not shed a single tear
i could choke down every family fight about money,
every caning that would come for no reason after those fights,
every time we were forced to go to my rich relatives for dinner and we'd
find ourselves in the kitchen cooking and doing the dishes.

i believed i knew the meaning of alcohol
i believed i knew how to get out of every single scrap
i believed i wasn't gonna make 25
i believed in 18 molecules of carbon
21 molecules of hydrogen
3 oxygen and one fab nitrogen
all in a sweet mixture enough to make me
feel like jennifer beals in *flashdance*
twirling my ass
in front of the snotty audition,
praying for a stinking place in
the dance-a-thon of actuality

back when my balls were the size of brazil
and my ego was the size of antarctica
and my courage was the size of phlegm
i learned to trust few people

learned to want little
and to need even less
i learned to say "FUCK IT"
with such ease and venom
the most cynical rattlesnake
would have its underbelly turn emerald
in two seconds flat.

you could wake to find yourself in some sweet danger,
in some piss-flavored version of addiction
designed to make up for lost time,
lost ideals, lost lovers, lost causes, lost saviours
but -shit- these days,
all i find is myself back when i was
back in the conga-line of perpetual desire
the territory of an incessant need
i crave my one habit of a good man
and i want to secede from
the grip of addiction philosophy,
from the colony of "i should've known better"

fuck that 12-step thing, i say,
i like to keep my options open
and i like having the option
to get absolutely fucked up
when i feel like it,
and not feel like i fucked up, dammit.

do things change that much?
can some stupid sign from the almighty
whip you right around?
maybe i should be looking for visions of jesus
in billboards of spaghetti sauce,
visions of buddha in men's semen,
maybe i'll be a much better person
if i knew who i was when i knew who i was
but who the fuck do i think i am?
i can't even piss straight into the bowl,
can't even tell my lover that i want to cook him

breakfast for the rest of my life,
can't even cross against the light,
    (ooh walk to the light, walk to the light...)
can't pay my bills on time nor balance my checkbook
can't dance, can't mosh,
can't get fucked up like i used to, not that i want to anyway
can't take it like a man, whatever that means.

all i can is kiss who i was
back when i knew who i was
goodbye, one great big tongue smooch
and wish him a good journey
as he walks to the light
and falls off the edge of earth
and into a peaceful hell.

I'll meet up with him later.

Lick My Butt

Lick the dry shit out of my sweaty buttcheeks

I've had my hepatitis shots so it's okay

Lick my butt
cos I'm an angry ethnic fag
& I'm in so much pain
so lick my butt

& the next time
when there's a multicultural extravaganza
& I'm asked for referrals
I can say
    "I know this guy,
    he's really cool,
    he licked my butt."

Lick my butt & tell me about
Michel Foucault's theories of deconstruction
& how it applies to popular culture,
a depressed economy & this overwhelming
tide of alienation.

Lick my butt from the center to the margins
& all the way back again.

Read Noam Chomsky in bed to me & lick my butt.

Lick my butt & give me my Prozac.
Lick my butt & call your mother, she misses you.
Flea-dip the cat & lick my butt.
Recycle & lick my butt.

Lick my butt like you really mean it.
Don't just put your tongue there
because you think it's something you should do
Do it cos you really really want to lick my butt.

My butt didn't always liked to be licked;
on the contrary, it hated anything wet
and sloppy, poking blindly
at its puckered dour grimace.
All it wanted was a nice pat,
an occasional squeeze,
a good warm seat and snug underwear.

It was happy with those,
but then all those other butts started
crashing in on its turf,
on the sidewalks and under my bed,
there were all these butts that said,
     no, demanded,
LICK ME.
My butt got tired of all that shit
& it just had to see what the fuss was all about.

At first it approached
the licking with extreme caution,
making sure all the checks
& balances were clearly present.

Hey — my butt had ever reason to be careful
it knows where it's been;
it's had enough of this bigotry
& poverty & violence
it's been on the wrong end of muggings & bashings
it's been working like a damn dog for years to make ends meet
it's been on the lam, on the block, on the contrary
& on sale for far too long

     so when that first slobber, smack,
slurp found its way into that
crack & up that uptight little asshole
it was like the Gay Pride Parade,
the Ice Capades, the Macy's Thanksgiving Day Parade
and Christmas happening all at once.

Now when I walk down the street
and you see me smiling
it's because I'm imagining
your tongue nestled in my buttcheeks
flicking away like a lizard
in a mad tweak.

Lick my butt & I'll lick yours;
we'll deal with shit of the world later.

Not ass but butt. Not kiss but lick. Something more playful (tender?) about "Lick My Butt" then "Kiss My Ass" (or "Fuck My Ass") in Justin Chin's imperative, wouldn't you say? A little trinity of monosyllables strung together to whet one's appetite for the anilingual orgy to come.

I remember when Manic D Press first brought out Justin's *Bite Hard* in 1996. I was looking for compatriots of the Gay Asian-American ilk. Tongzhi. In 2016, people are still talking about "Why are Asian women sexy but Asian men not?" Beyond institutionalized racism, sexism and homophobia, what are the alternatives to being seen as a merely exotic submissive sex object or an emasculated butt of tiny penis jokes?

This is a sidebar but fast forward to the film *Lost in Translation* where Bill Murray is trying to culturally navigate a hotel bedroom encounter with a Japanese prostitute who repeatedly shouts out: "LIP MY STOCKING! ... LIP MY STOCKING! ... LIP!," her native tongue's inability to produce the "R" sound in "RIP" an occasion for hilarity under the gaze of an implied white audience (myself included).

In the summer of 1990, I served not only as a waiter but as Donald Justice's teaching assistant. In a private conference going over a sheaf of my own poems, he remarked: "As a gay ex-Mormon Asian-American, the field is wide open, yours for the taking!" He then proceeded to extol the likes of Marilyn Chin, Li-Young Lee, Cathy Song, Garret Hongo, etc. There'd be a place for me at the table! I'm not sure what Donald would've made of Justin's lines.

Justin Chin's streetwise and subversively bossy top-to-bottom poetics flew under the radar of the Pink Literary Mafia (McClatchy & Co.). In Justin's poems, we witness categories such as the page (literary publishing) and the stage (spoken-word performance) start to collapse in a way that would've made Lana Turner proud had she lived to see the day.

Positivity

Waking to find red spots
on my chest and arms
and rushing to the bathroom
to get into better light
to see if the spots
are raised bumps
or wet crusting sores

only to find,
they are flea bites

Getting sick is not fun
anymore. It used to be
lying in bed reading
good books while listening
to the radio and pampering
myself with fruits and juices
and really good confectionery

Now, every red spot
and every swollen gland
worries me. I start feeling
my glands all day
thinking they are becoming bigger
every time I touch them,

and looking for lesions,
skip the vaccination scar
and the post-operative scar,
maybe they're just insect bites

Getting sick these days
prompts well-meaning friends
to call and ask how I'm doing,
when *was* the last time,
and just *what* did I do.

These Nervous Days

These nervous days,
I want to kiss you. I want to just kiss you & hold you. I want to kiss you &
hold you & hug you & love you & kill you. I want to kick my habit. I want to
open a border & close a bank. I want to open a mind & close a heart. I want
to open a shopping center & close a stadium. I want to have my own talk
show. Yeah I want a low-fat low-cholesterol guilt-free snack (cos I've got a
yummy yummy in my tummy tummy). I want a new gas mask. I want to be
the other white meat. I want to Deal-A-Meal. I want better weapons than
you. I want to kill more people than you. I want fuck more people than you.
I want to fuck over more people than you. I want better nipples. I want my
say even if I've got nothing to say. I want your new-age ritualistic karma
fuck-me-all. I want to kick your habit. I want to make you love me like
you love your dog. I want to meet Traci Lords and ask her why. I want to
meet Jeff Stryker and tell him to stop it. I want to be a buffed fag. I want to
discriminate against more people than you. I want to spread my brand of
hate-filled ideology with more venom than you. I want to spread more love
than your Mama. I want to know who's on first and why the fuck is he on
first and not me, dammit. I want to lick you butt, spread your asscheeks and
lick the dry shit out of your sweaty butthole. I want to swallow. I want to be
the last victim of cynicism, crucified on the cross of Fuck-You. I want to be
the first one to tell you.

And in these nervous days,
I want you to give me yr money. Give me yr spare change. Give me five. Give
me a break. Give me a better gig. Give me a minute. Give me a lifetime. Give
me yr mantra. Give me yr American history. Give me my American history.
Give me (gimme gimme) a man after midnight, won't somebody help me
chase the shadows away. Give me yr firstborn. Give me a hand. Give me just
a little more time. Give me God in a teacup. Give me God in a toilet duck.
Give me yr underpaid underemployed job. Give me this all ages show. Give
me a stiff drink. Give me a good beer. Give me hope. Give me the serenity to
accept the things I cannot change, the courage —oh fuck that shit—. Give
me shelter. Give me another chance, it's never happened before, I was just
tired. Give me another chance, I'm sorry I won't do that ever again. Give me
some cheap sentiment. Give me some sweet pain. Give me some chicken
tonight. Give me your tired, your weary, your huddled masses yearning to
breathe free. Give me yr cum, yr piss, yr spit. Give me yr infected blood.

Give me yr diseased genitals. Give me yr STDs. Give me yr best make-up tips. Give me yr secrets to clear skin, beauty, success & weight loss. Give me more power Scotty. Give me some sense of empowerment. Give me some sense of security. Give me yr best shot. Give me yr stinking crown. Give me more. Give me.

Give me what I ask for & you can take what you want from me.

Chinese Restaurant

I thought you'd like to know what really goes on in the kitchens of Chinese restaurants.

Well, when they say, "No M.S.G.," they're lying. When they say, "Tell us how hot & spicy," they really don't give a flying lizard fuck what you tell them, there's only one recipe, and you're going to eat it. And yes, they do spit into the food of the idiot, you know the one who everybody in the restaurant can hear: "How hot and spicy is that? Is it hot hot, or spicy hot, or chili hot, or garlic hot? It's not peppers, it is? Cos if it's too hot, I get a burning in my asshole when I shit." (Order the fucking steamed vegetables, buddy.) And yes, they do laugh quite unmercifully at the fool who actually tries to follow the pictorial instructions on how to use chopstick that's printed on the back of the chopstick wrapper. And just what the hell is Kung Pao, anyway?

In the kitchen of a Chinese restaurant they don't wash their hands much, but you already knew that. In the kitchen of a Chinese restaurant, someone is working way too hard for minimum wage but hey — it's a family thing, so it's okay and hey — it's America, where you make it if you work 12 hours a day, 7 days a week, so you can dream that American Dream, you know the one: where Diane Parkinson of *The Price Is Right* or Bob Barker of *The Price Is Right* spread it just for you. (Which one depends on your sexual orientation, No Substitutions Please. Unless, of course, you're Bi, then it's your lucky day.) Come On Down!

In the kitchen of a Chinese restaurant the waiter lives in fear of deportation, the dishwasher lives in fear of being bashed for stealing some stinking job nobody wants, the kitchen helper is scared to death of participating in the democratic political process & the chef knows someone who has AIDS at home or abroad.

From the kitchen of a Chinese restaurant I look for some semblance of the familiar. I look for home in every bite. In the dead spit of morning, after equal hours of "Silence=Death," "ACT-UP FIGHT BACK" & "What Do We Want? A Cure! When Do We Want It? Now!" I want some friendly solace & all I find is a lousy jerk-off, interrupted only by the 300-pound clerk who sticks his head through the door every ten minutes to yell, "Buy your tokens. Get into a booth or get out of here!"

I find no simple gesture can erase it all. I find a border that I cross each day for a decent wage of self-deception: call it optimism, call it a punch fuck, fist-fucking the ass of the quality of life (and it's a tight one too, baby.)

I find a pissant pleasure, a memoir of failure, cancer for brains. & I want to go, got to go, got to find this thing called home.

In the kitchen of a Chinese restaurant, I am queer for queer & I refuse to pass my ugliness for roses. I refuse to trade my queer for your queer.

At this point you're probably thinking, wait a minute, all of this wasn't in *The Joy Luck Club*; all this wasn't in the PBS special presentation, *A Thousand Pieces of Gold*, & all of this probably isn't in that stage production of *The Woman Warrior*, either.

But I just thought that you should know what goes on in the kitchens of Chinese restaurants.

Now go eat.

Justin Chin and I first met during the late spring of 1994 when I organized a one-night-only poetry slam: the winner would go on a paid multi-city summer tour with the Lollapalooza Festival. The Festival's third stage would be dedicated entirely to performance poetry. The slam was anonymous—participants picked random numbers from a hat—with the top scoring names revealed only at the end so that the judges would not be influenced by any writer's reputation or infamy. This sold-out decisive event was held on a weeknight at Slim's, a nightclub in San Francisco. More than 400 audience members were in attendance and 50 poets competed for this coveted chance to tour like a rock star as a paid poet, backstage pass and all.

After enduring a slew of seemingly endless 3-minute dramatic poetry pieces with varying degrees of merit, a slightly built young guy steps up to the mike and lauches into "Chinese Restaurant." It was one of those jaw-dropping moments where the audience couldn't believe what we were hearing.

First, he gets everyone laughing—the audience is fully on board with his sly pokes at familiar clichés and knowing caricatures—then WHAM! he lowers the boom, unfurls the sails, and there's the fierce yearning, stark vulnerability, profound emotional and political truths that no one saw coming but were so clear and real and present and undeniable. It was nothing less than astonishing. I think Justin got a standing ovation. Well, he definitely got one from me.

Justin did not win the slam that night; he placed second. But so began a literary friendship that lasted decades, and led to many books and readings and honors and subsequent adventures within San Francisco's writing community, which became over time an ersatz chosen family of sorts since (for a litany of reasons) we had all come here seeking to live our most authentic lives possible, as free from traditional societal constraints as any of us could muster. With grace and courage, Justin did just that.

Ex-Boyfriends Named Michael

My mother is concerned that I haven't met a nice boy to settle down with. She keeps asking me if I've met the right guy yet.

Well, Mom, there've been some nice guys who just didn't work out, some guys that have broken my heart, and there've been ex-boyfriends named Michael.

Ex-boyfriend named Michael #1 was a sheer mistake, but we make such delightful mistakes when we are young. You're supposed to learn from your mistakes, but heck...

Ex-boyfriend named Michael #2. I've washed him right out of my colon. Just for once, I'd like to date a man and not his therapist.

Ex-boyfriend named Michael #3 said I had communication problems, and I said, "Oh, go fuck yourself asshole." What I should have said was, "Honey, I am trying to understand your feelings of frustration at our seemingly inept articulations of our emotions, but I do have some unresolved feelings of anger towards you, so please go fuck yourself, asshole."

But maybe there's the off chance he's right. I have never been that great at communicating. Ex-boyfriend named Michael #4: I should have known better the first time we met and went back to his apartment to fuck. His idea of fuck music was Dan Fogelberg's *Greatest Hits*. I asked him to change the CD, and he changed it to the only thing that could have been worse: *Neil Diamond Live at Madison Square Garden*.

Coming to America, indeed.

But I stuck with him and every fuck at his place was sheer hell. I tried telling him that his taste in music sucked and that I could seriously help him, but somehow I lacked the communication skills to do just that. But then I thought I loved him, and then I was young enough and foolish enough to believe that love can overcome Linda Ronstadt.

It cannot.

But love did not stop me from throwing his Yanni CDs behind the bookcase nor did it stop me from torching his *Ballads of Madison County* CD on the gas stove. Oh, what a beautiful blaze it was! He swore the CD was a gift but like all ex-boyfriends named Michael, he was a lying dog. Now I'm getting ahead of myself here, that's about creatively destroying ex-boyfriends' property, not about ex-boyfriends named Michael.

Ex-boyfriend named Michael #5 was suffering from a severe case of yellow fever and dumped me for some little Taiwanese guy, fresh off the damn boat. Two weeks in the Yoo-Ass and the little pissant faggot manages to find his way to Cafe Hairdo, ready to be picked up by his American Dream of Homosexual Romance. I can just see him sitting there, legs crossed, working his non-threatening little Third World charm, offering to share his table and newspaper. I can just see them now: sharing haircare products, making mutual consensual decisions about dinner, movie, sex and their emotional well-beings. I can see them sitting on the sofa with the dictionary in their laps trying to figure out the difficult words in Barbara De Angelis' *Making Love Work* video seminar, and thinking about adopting a fox terrier named Honey. I can see them having deep, deep discussions about which one of them has a better butt:

"You do."

"You do."

"No, you do."

"Stop it! You do."

"Yours is tight and tanned."

"But your is pert and angry."

What a pair of goddamn fucking freaks. I would just like to see them in a big car accident crashing into an oncoming truck carrying a shipment of Ginzu kitchen knives.

But hey, I'm not bitter, I'm descriptive. I'm not jaded. I just have too many ex-boyfriends named Michael.

Just once, I'd like to see everything of my life with ex-boyfriends named Michael laid out on a fat barge sent off to the landfill of affection. I'll watch the barge ferry it's way through the flotsam of therapy & crabs, dishsoap & bad sex, shared shirts & worry, devotion & drugs, pissed-off nights & legless drunken revelry.

I'll wave goodbye and I'll be fine.

Chicken Little

With the sky fallen,
with my tail feathers drooped and flumped
I stand at the edge of the great pit,
matched only by the one in my stomach
grinding by my gizzards.
In the cineplex, I'm a hero,
saving the world from annihilation,
but here, I'm just some diseased cluck.
Why us? Why do the canaries,
the sparrows and pigeons, the parakeets
get a free ride? If only you knew
what those pretty songbirds hide
in their diseased throats, under their pretty
feathers. And it's more than a sniffle,
or a flu, I can tell you that.

At daybreak, they will round up all my kind,
herd them into this great hole, pour bags of lime over them
disregarding the panic, and push dirt in, bury them
alive. When the boots and tractors and gawkers are gone,
who will hear the turned soil's muted cluckering?
Tell me again the sky hasn't fallen.
But that is the lot of my peeps.
We face fire. We always have.
Unfortunately, when we pass through fire,
we become fantastically tasty.

Refuging

I.
Where is my refuge,
my fine and feathered friend?
Sitting in the blue glow
of the steam room
where men pass each other
like ghosts, silent,
suspicious, surveying
and strapped for some
humanness, I look through
the billowing wisps
of vapor to the man
standing at the door.
His strong limbs, all
I ever knew how to lean on,
His broad brown body, all
the touch I ever remember;
How often I have wanted him,
to feel his warm spit
against mine,
and to smell his fleshy need.
And if I never saw his face
again, I will know I last saw it,
handsome as ever,
passport size in the back pages of a newspaper.
And while I chase his shadow
down dimly lit hallways
with sticky floors
and sounds of other men
finding their bits of godsend,
I find that I do not show
up in a mirror anymore.
I have become yet another ghost,
like Caspar, friendly
and unselective.

Where is my refuge,
my fine and feathered friend?
In the smoke of the woodfire oven,
the smells of roast pork and chicken,
the chipping of ice blocks,
the popping of Anchor beer for the adults,
Pepsi for the kids,
and the clacking of mah jong tiles,
I watch my family at reunion.
Uncles and aunts prying into
each other's children
secretly comparing notes.

Where is my refuge, my fine
and feathery friend?
Hiding in the space
in which I loved you,
and the body
in which I find you,
demands it.

Where
is my refuge, my fine,
and festive friend,
from the roles of filial
concern inbred
through centuries
of parent and child
cycles of the necessity of home?
And while I hear the static of long
distance phone calls and air letters,
all caught between come and stay;
but homes and familial comforts
hold nothing in this court
of duty, shame
and responsibility.

Where is my refuge,
my worn and weary friend,

from the men who loved me,
from the myths and philosophies
thrust upon me and my race?
Where is my refuge from the belief
that I will live to a hundred and five
that I will never get cancer,
nor high blood pressure
nor heart disease?
Where is my refuge from the men
who say, "I don't really like Asians
but they're so much safer to fuck
these days"?

Where
is my refuge,
my fine, my feathery,
my worn, my weary friend?

II.
When his lover fell,
he carried his man, his brother,
his life on his back
and dashed out into the foggy
rancid early morning freeze;
but the 5 a.m. cabs would not stop
because two Asian men
unsure on their legs
one draped over the other's shoulder
lifeless and shivering, both
looking pissed drunk and frantic
look like trouble,
you never know which gangs you'll fall foul of
this side of Chinatown
if you pick them up.

Falling into the E.R. of St. Mark's
he comes face to face,
with the clerk, moonly white,
glowing Jesuslike

in his standard issue hospital gown, who says
"You have to take him to St. Luke's
we don't speak your language here,"
and he shuts the window
in a silent movement of the hand,
quiet and final
as the two men whose combined weights equaled
not the balance of language,
the difference,
nor the truth of any matter,
slouch into the Dettoled floor,
silent, angry,
and dying.

III.
Touch the ground.
Feel the stubble of the newly grown
crab grass creeping across the earth,
damp from December rains.
This is the feel of a man I once loved.
Kneeling on the ground,
the wetness seeps through my jeans
marking two wet spots.
I wish I had flowers,
some marigolds, carnations and irises,
to put on the ground to break the monotony
of wet soil and another Human Services burial.
What's the use of sobbing over a metal plant label,
so washed out you can't even read the name,
much less the date of birth or the date
it all ended?

Sometimes, I call your number
knowing that it has been disconnected
for months. I want the reassurance
of the recorded message telling me that.
Often, I slam the receiver down after the second ring,
heart pounding, afraid
that someone might actually answer.

No one will. Silence
invents a belief that holds solidly
to memories. The feel of your body,
its sweat-salt taste, the musty smell
of cigarette smoke in your hair,
all silenced, replaced.

Nowadays, people I don't know call
to tell me how sorry they are.
Bill calls and says it was a nice funeral.
I meet him later in the bar,
vodka-tonic in his hand,
he saunters over to tell me
I really shouldn't be alone
at a time like this.
"I'll drive you home," he says,
and I remember his absence
on the end of the line
when I called him
after you called me
to tell me you were halfway
dying. Not that he wasn't there,
he just didn't want to speak to me
in the presence of his boyfriend
because that would be tricky.
So I went to the supermarket
because I did not want to be alone
and that did not help,
so I ran as far as I could.
Across the ocean, all the way
to New Orleans. There,
drunk half-assed out of my mind,
I wished you were with me
when I fucked the Belizean dope dealer
while his sister slept
in the same room behind a screen.

Walking in some nameless graveyard
at 3 a.m., feeling the wet grass

on my soles, feeling unpinned down
and invisible,
I came back.
Cleared the board.
Started life from GO.
I've been around the board
so many times, I've lost count
and you in the process.
But I'm here now.
And I know where you are.

IV.
Where is my refuge,
my wise and worldly friend?
Where is it?

V.
Continuing Miss Saigon,
    "Tonight the heat is on."
The first boats fresh
from fire in the Gulf
descend on Pataya, Bangkok
for some R&R. The men have all been given
rubbers and watched safe sex videos
before being let loose on the
available and waiting brown boys and girls
patient for their American G.I. dreams
of hard dicks and U.S. dollars,
and any one from this batch
of seventy thousand odd
can bring hope
of Hollywood movie romance:

        Mel Gibson meets innocent native
        boy, falls in love with his pure
        virgin fuck and after being shipped away,
        comes swimming back across the ocean
        to bring him across the Pacific to live
        in the splendor of Rodeo Drive,

Fifth Avenue and American Express.

While over at the Rome Club,
the boys, prancing on stage
like a buffet for the Europeans
with big hearts and bigger wallets,
— though everyone knows a few dollars
goes a long way here —
are wearing their
Don't be silly - Put a condom on your willy
t-shirts, courtesy of some American foundation.
As they gyrate and touch their slim bodies
in front of appreciative sex tour loads,
dreaming of love and economics,
none asks what the shirt says,
nor do the few who do speak English
have an idea what a willy is;
these are costumes assigned
by the Boss Man, and whatever gets
the customers is what works,
but the white woman smiling self-satisfied
at the side of the stage can now go home
and sleep safe and happy
knowing that she saved
some third world natives
from themselves,
as each of them disappears,
as the night drags on,
into the back room
or, if they're really lucky,
into the warm Hilton or Sheraton
where maybe even breakfast awaits them,
as they disappear
as the nights drag on.

VI.
Some days, just leave.
Just pack it all up.
Let them tow away your car.

Let the plants die.
Let the cat run away.
Let your shiny white bicycle rust away.
Some days, just go.
Leave it all behind.
Death is the only way out,
now that alcohol has failed
and AA meetings are meaningless
as coffee and doughnuts.
The appetite is gone.
Don't have any urges
anymore, except maybe
to start again.
But you can't do that.
The half life of this body
is short. Nothing
is immune, anymore.
The banquet table is spread.
Pick at the food,
maybe it'll feed
this dying body
struggling to find a life, a way out
of the pain of knowing
living can never be the same,
not when you have the terminal bug.
Sometimes, you just got to
kiss it all away, let go,
once and for all,
lie back, and maybe wait
for the peace to come
or not.

VII.
Where is my refuge,
my wonderful and wintry friend?
Where do I find it?

VIII.
When a voice finally speaks
across the void of stillness,
how many of us will be gone,
how many will I have left,
committed to picture memories
and the mind feel of touch
against my body?
Fingerprints ingrained to my flesh
and smells that hit me
when I let my guard down
during silence, the meniscus
of nothingness
that cannot be broken.
Not even by the passionate fist punching
air shouts of "Silence = Death."
Nor the falseness of a Queer Nation,
the lie of Brotherhood,
or the bigger lie of "G.W.M. G.B.M. G.L.M. G.A.M."
Decibels mean nothing playing
in the numbers racket.
Palm up, odds
slimmer than the lottery
cut across the whole U.S. of A.
What makes you say
"Pick a number
and I will prove you wrong"?
Existing in numbers that don't measure up
and comforting ourselves
in this belief, waiting
for the quiet to fall dead around some ankles
before anyone even notices.

I try to be fearless.
I try to be numb
and always
I'm back where I started.
And everyday a new refuge is lost.
My grief cannot turn angels to gods,

nor can it tear demons from men.
All it does is hold me down, quiet,
to nights when nothing speaks
and nothing is light
as mildew lifting.

IX.
Where is my refuge?
Give me refuge,
O watchful,
O warrant friend.

I could never tell when Justin was telling the truth. It's not that he was a liar; it was just that he was a helluva storyteller. It may be instructive to know that once when Justin was critiquing a piece of my writing, he cried out, "Oh gawd, have you never heard of fiction?"

The first piece of Justin's writing I ever heard was when he read "Refuging" at a fundraiser. The odd thing is that at the time Justin and I had been living together as boyfriends for about six months. The flat at 17th and Church was his first Bay Area home when he transferred from University of Hawaii to San Francisco State. I had asked repeatedly to see his writing, but he refused every time. So I was in the audience, listening from the back of the room, and felt like I was being punched in the guts. How could I not know that this 21-year-old cutie sharing my bed could write with such enormous power? I knew Justin was smart, damn smart. And I knew about his wicked wit (so often aimed at me). But I didn't know he could use words to create such vivid imagery and heartfelt emotion.

Following the reading I had questions: "Was that about you? That part where one guy is helping his friend and they can't get a taxi to stop and then the scene at the emergency room...?" His answers were always noncommittal. Was Justin writing from his own experience? Or was this something that happened to friends of his? Or was it just something he'd heard about? I never got an answer.

In time I understood that the source of that truth didn't matter. Justin's truth was incisive and sharply expressed. That story reflected on Justin's experiences of homophobia in Malaysia and Singapore, and the racism he experienced in America. It reflected on the sadness he saw all around him in the Castro of the early '90s.

Justin's imagery and storytelling were in service of his own pain, his own outrage at the world, his own unhappiness. I know that Justin was writing the truth when he said, "The half life of this body is short. Nothing is immune, anymore."

And now a quarter century later I find myself asking, "Where is my refuge my wonderful and wintry friend? Where do I find it?" And once again I know I will never get an answer.

Sleepless

See what goes on at night: Animals with flashing eyes walk on stilts carrying broken beer bottles; trees grow ears and lips and vulvas and sneak into your bed, slide under your covers; cockroaches and slugs metamorphosize into fat-free low-cholesterol pound cakes.

People who can't sleep don't have eyelids, or can't close them like fish and birds. People who can't sleep are destined to die with their eyes open. They know this and they obsessively watch TV shows where the actors sleep and dream and wake; and at every commercial break, they use the full force of their palms, sweaty from being clenched so long and tight, to push their elastic eyelids down, but the lids just won't close; it's as if they were rusty, exposed to sea air for too long, defective.

In real life, people who die with their eyes open can watch their funeral, their cremation; they will witness their bodies burning and their unclosed eyes popping in the hellish heat of the crematorium oven like chestnuts on hot coals. If they opt for the old-fashioned, they will watch their bodies slowly rotting in varnished sandalwood coffins until the muscle and tissue holding their uncovered eyes are devoured by mites and ants, and their ever-bugged eyes fall with a dull clank into hollowed skulls like marbles hitting the bottom of an empty fishbowl.

People who can't sleep do not have nightmares of violence; no dreams of hoofed or horned animals or root vegetables scheming to slice open their fat blue veins with the kitchen knife the moment they fall asleep; they never sleep afraid that other people who can't sleep will hurt them when they sleep. And when they wake from sleeplessness, the new day drags like old paint over their ever more cruel and pitiful skin, as if their aching flesh were merely a sad dream, remembered with utmost clarity, from an innocent childhood.

Night

The light from the street lamp shines
through the window and shades your face.
In this dull shadow, you look different,
disfigured like the gargoyles I saw
at the museum today; it was
a visiting exhibition, next week
there will be something from South America.

As you sleep, cradled in my body,
your breathing is rhythmic. Listening
to your soft breath, I breathe
in time with you, counting the number
of breaths each minute, 17.

You look so small when
you're asleep. I wonder
what you're dreaming, and if you'd remember
the dream when you wake.

I dreamed of Dorothy Parker.
She came to me and said *bitch*; then
spiders gathered around me. Dorothy
Parker was wearing a dress with spider prints
on it. I thought it was curtain material.
I woke and saw your monster features
tucked in me and I was frightened. I
wanted to scream but did not want to wake you.

The clock glares its red eyes at me
and says *sleep*.
I glare back and say *count the time, count*.
The clock says *I will*.

A woman looks in from the window,
she doesn't say a word; I think
she is crying. She stands and we look
at each other for a while before she melts

into the shape of a spider on the window,
lost, homeless, and probably hungry.

I offer it my blood to suck but it declines;
it only wants blood from flying organisms.
I cannot fly
even if in dreams I flew
off a tall blue building, listening
to Patsy Cline records. I glided
for a while, then plummeted to my sheets,
wet and shivering.

The cat enters the room, looks
at us. He jumps on the bed, licks his paws
and smiles at me like he knows something
I don't. He winks at me, blows me a kiss, moves
to the window, kills the spider with a swat
of his paw, yawns and disappears through the window.
I see him flying upward, soaring like
a plastic toy aeroplane.
He tells me of the neighborhood
in the darkness of the nearly morning,
the little contained in each shoebox, all
kitty litter, all waiting
for the morning, to
be taken all away.

Daniel Handler

The poems I like best hit me like sharp thoughts—worry or dread or fear or complication—late at night in bed. It's a magical, blue-lit space, but it's a troubling one too; everything looks kind of beautiful but I'm too spooked to enjoy it. The mysterious looping of thoughts, the weird sidetracks and the jarring revelations: it's the stuff of insomnia, of a half-conscious brain alert with the intangible, and it's those moments in poetry I love.

"Night" has this quality in abundance; it's also the subject of the poem, the feeling of drifting in and out of sleep, in and out of anxiety, late at night. It's audacious to try to write a poem about wandering thoughts (everybody knows you're supposed to take your wandering thoughts and shape them into a poem) – it's the sort of writing some people call "risky," as if the dangers of failing in poetry have anything to do with the corporeal dangers of walking through life.

The first stanza is basically perfect. I mean look at where it moves: We start out the window, then next to us in bed, then there's a gargoyle in the shadows, then across town in a museum, a few hours previous, then the future, then South America. And yet the lines move so cleanly; it's just the way we fall asleep, our little brains gripping some little slice and then suddenly we're miles away. The poem keeps it up all night, floating through spare sweetness ("You look so small when / you're asleep") and banal fact-finding ("counting the number / of breaths each minute, 17"), wacky dream logic ("Dorothy / Parker was wearing a dress with spider prints"), ghostly visitations ("She stands and we look / at each other for awhile before she melts / into the shape of a spider on the window") until it's morning, or nearly morning: thoughts of morning, anyway, those everyday thoughts that prickle in as the night flips to daytime.

I loved this poem when I first read it—September '05, according to the scrawled autograph—and I've returned to it before, trying to steal its secrets, but giving up and just reading it for that prickly feeling it gives me. It's a perfect little marvel, like so much of Justin Chin's stuff: it feels almost offhand but it hits like a pro. And I've been thinking about this poem lately, now that the poet is gone, this poem that moves like time passing, fast and slow, in all directions. Justin and I shared a stage once or twice; we had people in common; we exchanged maybe a dozen words. I thought we'd end up knowing each other someday. I thought we had time, and then he was gone.

What I Did Last Summer

Bite Hard, my book of poetry, had finally come out and it was time to whore it. Beth Lisick, who had written the utterly faboo *Monkey Girl*, published by the same press as I, was going to chuck her workaday routine, climb into her dad's truck (hers got stolen), and go on a mondo road trip, traveling to thirty-odd cities in seven weeks, doing readings and selling books out of the back of her truck. It's like Anne Rice's bus tour but without the bus, the budget, the coffin, or the legions of Goth kids trailing along. I was to accompany her on the southern leg of her tour.

I have had my own preconceived notions about the southern part of the country. Informed by movies and especially TV (*Dukes of Hazzard, BJ and the Bear*, and its spin-off *Lobo*), I expected hillbillies, rednecks, twangy accents, big hair, country music, humorless Christians, and KKK rallies around every corner.

Even before that, weeks before, I had gone to upstate New York to hang out at my friend Ames' little cabin in West Exeter, located somewhere near the town of Winfield. I think it's all close to Utica, but I'm not sure. He drove.

California and New York are those states that people have very definite ideas about. Say "California," and people immediately think of Hollywood, sunny beaches, cable cars chugging down the Golden Gate Bridge, and *Baywatch*. Truth be told, California is huge, and outside of the bigger cities, the state is a massive sprawling suburb, and then massive sprawling farms, peopled with migrant farm workers.

Say "New York," and people think of New York City, maybe *NYPD Blue*, Broadway, and Times Square, even that movie. But here way out along the interstates, New York looks like central California, like the Midwest, like the farm belt. Lots of dairy and cow farms dotting the landscape. If those militant vegetarians want people to stop eating meat, they should just bottle up the smell of those darn cow farms and the gallons of cow poop.

Ames suggested we go to the VFW for their annual Labor Day barbecue. "VFW, are you mad?" I said. "You want me to go to a place filled with veterans, whose proudest, most crowning moment was defending their country from people who look like me, and have possibly killed a whole bunch of people who look like me and might still be possibly having flashbacks?" But the price was right and so we went. The old veterans were cordial and nice, the barbecue was good shit. And the most I got was a lot of stares, some more discreet than others.

Yup, America is white. Recent reports in the media might suggest that the country was being overrun by all these dusky people. Immigrants dashing across the border like the Roadrunner, swimming ashore on rickety boats, and sneaking into airports, stealing all those great garment factory, janitorial, and agricultural jobs that the pure-blooded American high-schoolers all so desperately want and have been training ten years for. And then on *Cops*, it's always the colored folks that are being chased and clobbered. And on non-"Reality TV" (ha!), the colored folks are still being clobbered by the good cops.

But if you look at the last census report, the country is still 80 percent white, which is a heck of a lot of white, though probably not enough for some folks.

We started our trip in Austin, where I was to meet Beth. She had already been driving all down California through the Southwest and through west Texas.

At the Austin airport I'm whisked off by Hillary, our host and a fellow poet, to do a spot on a local radio show. I'm cautioned about using those seven words, but unfortunately I only know four of those seven words. I read a sweet love poem (no swearing, no fucking), ending it by making some silly comment about how I wished the person it was written for (who had since left) would come to a bitter end.

"Oh no!" Nancy, the radio host with her soothing melted-margarine voice says earnestly. "You must think of love as like a meteorite, that just burns and passes by."

"Yeah, I hope the meteorite will crash into his apartment," I say.

"Oh no!" Nancy and Gayle, her cohost, simultaneously chirp in wide-eyed disapproval. "It's best to move on from a failed relationship," Gayle offers helpfully.

"Now let's hear some music from Namibian bushwomen. I've always wondered what Namibian bushwomen sound like, haven't you?" Gayle says.

"No, I can't say I know what Namibian bushwomen sound like!" Nancy banters back. Hillary and I leave to the chants of Namibian bushwomen.

We head on to the local bookstore where we are to do an afternoon reading. Two people show up for the reading, one of them had gone to high school with Beth. Beth accidentally smashes the bookstore's little clip-on mike. Austin was spent going to the local swimming hole, a creek that the municipality had dammed up to make a nice cool natural swimming pool, going to clubs and watching bands, drinking loads of beer and enjoying the company, the charms and the hospitality of the locals. In Austin, I discovered the difference between chicken fried steak, chicken fried chicken, and just fried chicken. Chicken fried steak is mainly chicken beaks, feet, and gizzards, shaped into a patty and fried. (Well, it's actually ground beefsteak.) Chicken fried chicken is a moist breast of chicken battered and fried (good eating with ranch dressing). And fried chicken is a hunk of chicken with bone that is battered and fried.

We leave Austin late at night. The roads are less crowded, and the air is less stifling. It is right smack in the middle of summer, and the heat and humidity are unrelenting. The dust from the freeways and the sticky, clammy air we have to drive through are brutal. The plan is to drive until Beth passes out, then we'll look for a cheap motel. Beth has to do all the driving since I don't drive. Not well, at least. She's real cool about it, and I try to pull my weight by reading the maps and navigating. In the cool night air, accompanied by drive-time radio, we pass Waco and Dallas, two places that have made their mark on television sets all over the world. All I know of Dallas is several seasons of the said soap opera. In one early episode, Lucy Ewing, the spoiled niece, is angry at the family. It is her sweet sixteen birthday, and the Ewings are throwing a huge party for her at Southfork. But Jock refuses to allow Lucy to invite her mother, and JR is using the party to make business deals. Lucy is furious and runs off to Waco to look for her mother. Along the way, she is kidnapped by a handsome drifter who robs diners. He makes her sing "Silver Threads and Golden Needles" at a local bar's amateur hour while he robs the place. Then Bobby rescues her. But this was before anyone, except for some ATF agents, knew what was going on in Waco. In the weekday night, Waco is still and quiet and an eerie air hangs over the place. We drive with the windows down and the wind whips through the car with noisy delight. I imagine what it must have been like on the night when the Davidian compound was burnt down, how the air, thick with dark smoke, must have smelled.

Places that we think are chains, like Red Lobster and Sizzler, are actually regional things. Here, they're pretty much the same things but with different unfamiliar names. But it's basically the same fried chicken, the same burgers, the same pizzas, and the same fried seafood joint. We drive past a couple of Hooters, and Beth and I conspire to go there sometime and I will play her retarded charge. Clutching my Human Anatomy coloring book, we'll go in pretending that we think that Hooters is a theme restaurant about owls. "Where are the owls, Aunty Beth?" I'll ask in my Lenny from *Of Mice and Men* on-TNT-movies voice. I imagine that Hooters will have waitresses whose heads turn a little more than 180 degrees as they survey the floor asking, "Who? Who? Who ordered the margarita?" And when we leave, we will buy the Hooters' clip from the gift shop. This is a clip that you use on the back of your T-shirt so that it will pull your T-shirt snugly over the front of your torso. But of course, we simply end up at Whattaburger.

Next stop: Fayetteville, Arkansas. Along the way, after we cross the Oklahoma border, we stop for lunch at a small, greasy, wood shack roadside diner. The diner is filled with old men and women, and the old guy sitting in the booth behind us is wearing a faded T-shirt that proudly proclaims "I Am the NRA." There is a pastel airbrushed painting of John Wayne's head hovering over a herd of galloping horses on the wall. I realize what a sight Beth and I must make. She's wearing a halter top, midriff showing, and her hair is an iridescent purple; and I'm tattooed down three-quarters of my arms and so obviously not the chinky from the local Chinese restaurant.

The drive to Fayetteville is scenic, a lot of mountains and crafts shops. We keep thinking we should stop for googly-eyed almond tabletop knickknacks as souvenirs but keep our urges in check and drive on. We drive past a nuclear reactor and it looks like it does in movies: two cylindrical concrete top hats surrounded by a huge pond, ominously lurking over the lush green countryside. One of the tourist attractions of the Ozarks is the Jesus of the Ozarks. Some zealous Christians decided that they wanted to build a statue of Jesus to rival the one in Rio de Janeiro. What better way to show their love for our Lord and Savior than by erecting an epic Jesus, arms outstretched to receive his flock? Only problem was that they had originally built it too high and had to cut the poor Lord off at the knees, so the Jesus of the Ozarks looks like a stumpy midget Christ. And he has a red light on the top of his holy head to warn planes of his blessings.

In Fayetteville, I'm sitting by the bar at the club we are about to read at. The locals are all excited, and the local poetry slam team are out to help bring in an audience for us. I'm sitting at the bar nursing my beer and going over what I will read. It's always tough to know how much queer an audience can take. Should I do the cocksucker piece? the fist-fucking piece? A tall thin handsome grizzled man comes up to me. "Are you Justin?" he asks, and I tell him that I am. "This is for you," he says, and gives me a small bunch of wildflowers and a card, inside which is written: *The queer and faerie communities welcome you to the Ozarks.* Yes, I think I will read the cocksucking and fist-fucking pieces tonight!

We meet up with Brenda, a local writer, whose day job is home-care provider. She takes care of AIDS patients in Fayetteville. When she talks about her work, it surprises me at first. After close to twenty years of the AIDS epidemic, and the constant reminders that AIDS is not merely a disease in the big cities, and all that, it still takes me by surprise when I realize that there are untold numbers of people who are living in this country who have AIDS but do not have the ready and overwhelming access to drugs, services, information, and a community as we do in San Francisco or New York. They've traded all that for home, or what they know as home. That people actually do "go home to die," and that families do take care of their sick children, and old friends do care.

Our next day in Fayetteville, our host Lisa takes us shooting in Hogeye with her boyfriend, who may or may not have ties to the Ozarks militia. We nip into the gun shop to buy bullets, and I am amazed how cheap bullets are, a mere fiver for a box of thirty-six, such a deal. The gun shop is also a pawnshop and they have a dazzling display of pro-NRA, anti-Clinton bumper stickers. We drive up to Lisa's boyfriend's cabin. His family has lived on the mountain for the last five or so generations. It's like the Waltons but with lots of guns. Greg has saddled up the horses for us and we ride up to the top of the mountain to shoot up tree stumps. Greg has broken out his cache of cop-killer bullets, the ones with the armor-piercing inner core for us to use. We protest—since these bullets are now illegal, we don't want him to waste it on us greenhorns. But he graciously lets us shoot them. We start with a nice Magnum, firing it into a cross section of a felled tree.

I was so Kelly Garrett. I had never held a real gun before, much less fired one, but amazingly I hit all my targets that day. The first blast from the gun was incredible: the ringing in my ears, the ricochet jerking my arm back. Beth and I were amazed that we knew how to ride horses and shoot guns just from watching TV. All those episodes of *Dynasty* when Krystle went riding on Allegria at Delta Rho Farms sure helped. After firing off the Magnum, we head back down to the cabin to fire off Chinese-made AK-47s and shotguns. The AK-47s were great. "The gun that won the Vietnam War!" Greg tells us, as he shows us how to attach the massive bayonet to the tip of the gun and how to thrust it into someone's stomach. It's very Rambo. The AK-47s are semiautomatic things that just crack and spew bullets all over the place, no kickback, no fuss, easy as turning on the faucet. It's the postal worker's wet dream. You can't have a clip that contains more than thirty bullets, but Greg shows us how to duct-tape another clip to the existing one so that you can change the clip in a blink. Later, back in the car and on the road again with Beth, I confess that the Vietnam War comment had me really uncomfortable. After all, who was the gook in this whole show-and-tell here? "I just bit my tongue and didn't say anything," I said.

"He didn't say that we won the war, he said it was the *gun* that won the war, and I guess maybe the Vietcong had the Chinese-made guns," Beth offers.

The shotguns proved to be more of a challenge. Still, Beth and I knew how to reload the shotgun from watching Linda Hamilton in *Terminator 2*. Damn, I was butch. We fired off the shotguns at paper plates and again, I hit all my targets. Beth was having a more difficult time. "Try to relax," Greg advises. "You seem so tense."

"Maybe it's because I have a huge gun in my hands," Beth replies. Still, in a bikini and with that gun, she would be any militia guy's choice pinup for all the long months holed up in his mountain cabin waiting for the ATF raid.

Shooting guns is quite addictive and the power of it is undeniable: Once the bullet leaves the barrel, it will go its way in split seconds and there is nothing to stop it.

Beth and I leave Fayetteville and drive through the Ozarks. Next stop: Memphis.

You cannot go to Memphis and not go to Graceland. Like most monumental buildings, Graceland is smaller than I expect. The plaza is across from the mansion and we dutifully buy our tickets. We're only going to do the house tour, skipping the garage and plane tour both of which will cost extra. Graceland is filled with older doughy white-trash tourists, and young Japanese tourists, the ones who are endlessly enamored of Americana and will buy all those Confederate flags and decorate with them without really understanding what they mean. In line to board the bus that will take us across the street to Graceland proper, we spy an older woman who's wearing a tank top so she can flaunt the young Elvis postage stamp tattoo on her free-flabbing sausage arms.

We get out the headsets for the audio tour of the mansion and we are off. Beth and I are terrified that we might actually say something that may be perceived to be irreverent and get beat up by the devotees and kicked out of Graceland. The tour starts with the living room and the dining room. Everything is cheesy sixties and seventies over-the-top metallic art deco meets rococoan psychedelia psychodrama. The tour proceeds through the kitchen and into the rec room. It's gorgeous. The room is done up in yards upon yards of pleated batik fabric from floor to ceiling. We go to the Jungle Room, famous for its green-shag carpeting among other things. Elvis used to record in this room, and apparently the shag helps the acoustics. In spite of a segment on *House of Style*, I never knew how to use shag carpeting on the walls until now. I am disappointed that we are not allowed onto the second floor. I so much wanted to see the bedrooms and the bathrooms (what kinds of toiletries? what kind of loo rolls?). Then it's off to the offices, the stables (converted into museum), and the annex where all the gold records, awards, and costumes are housed. Elvis was quite enamored of law enforcement and had even offered to spy for the FBI. A nice note from J. Edgar Hoover politely turning down his offer is framed and hung on the wall. Elvis was also quite taken by Eastern mysticism, martial arts, and religions. His nunchaks and ninja paraphernalia are displayed. Another surprise since Elvis is always represented as the ultimate all-American icon, worshiping God and country, and recording albums full of hymns. In fact, all his Grammys (on display too) were for his gospel recordings. Elvis's costumes are also displayed. I had only seen them on the man himself, as he sashayed across the TV screens, on video, and in countless photographs. But here, they were tacked to the wall like mounted butterflies. It all just seems so unreal.

The audio tour is also terribly reverent to the King. Sample: "Soon, life on the road took its toll. Elvis developed health problems." "He and Priscilla separated, but they still remained loving parents to little Lisa Marie…" and "That was the last concert Elvis gave. Later that afternoon, he passed away." All of these translates to: He took loads of drugs and got fat, he didn't want to fuck Priscilla after she dropped the bun, and he had a heart attack while trying to squeeze out a U-Blocker on the loo.

The tour ends at the Eternal Flame, where the graves of Elvis and his parents are. People are weeping and taking photos. Devotees leave flowers, cards, teddy bears, and little mementos which the estate assures will be either saved for the archives or sent to children's hospitals.

Then it's back to Graceland the mall to buy postcards, fridge magnets, and all sorts of Elvis-related stuff. I send my mom some little souvenirs. She is a big Elvis fan, and family stories have it that her father actually tossed her Elvis record out of the window when she first played it in the house.

The reading in Memphis goes well. We read at the P&H Cafe, which is run by Wanda, a boisterous Janis Joplin-esque lady who wears big hats and sasses everyone. In Memphis, too, we partake of our first taste of Memphis pork sandwiches. By this time, my affinity toward pork is well evident, and I'm trying to keep my servings of pork down to six a week. It's difficult but I try.

We leave Memphis and drive through Mississippi, stopping at a small motel in the wee hours of the morning. A lot of the small motels are independently owned and operated by South Asians, we find. The next morning, we drive into Birmingham, Alabama, and we stop in the city center to look at the sculpture garden. A small walkway around the park takes us from one huge brass sculpture to another depicting the civil-rights struggle. In the summer, there's a water hose actually spraying a sculpture of civil-rights protesters. One of the most terrifying sculptures is of police dogs attacking two little Black children. The detail captured in the brass is amazing, and the looks on the children's faces and the ferocity of the dogs are powerful.

Standing in that park on that summer afternoon, I feel the weight of history. That on that very soil, thirty some years ago, all this heroism, passion, anger, courage, and fear came head to head with hatred and intolerance. A few months later, I will find myself in Dallas at the Texas School Book Depository and wandering around Dealey Plaza, and I will feel that same sense of weight. I wonder if younger queer kids will one day look at streets where ACT UP and Queer Nation protested during those Reagan-Bush years and feel that same weight.

Throughout our road trip, I keep looking out for other Asians, and apart from the South Asians we rent the motel rooms from and later in Atlanta, I hardly see any on the streets. The only sign of anyone Asian comes from the Chinese restaurants that we pass. They are all named nonthreateningly and catering to that sense of Western orientalia: Golden Wok, House of Won Ton, Potsticker Palace, China House "Home of the $4.99 Buffet," The Fortune Cookie, and Chop Suey Palace.

After much driving, we make it to our destination: Athens, Georgia. Athens was one of those magical places of college rock that existed in my mind. In Athens, we are going to stay with Marie, an older Southern socialite, who is a friend of a friend of Beth's. She is beautiful, gracious, and utterly charming. And her house is amazingly beautiful. It was built in the 1850s and a new annex was added on in the 1890s to bring the kitchen indoors. The floors are interlaced with oak and maple hardwoods so that they are striated, and the place is beautifully decorated with antique furniture. We sleep in four-poster beds with good linen and well-padded mattresses, such a change from crashing on people's couches and sleeping in cheap, dinky motels. Usually, Beth and I give our hosts our books as a token of our appreciation for putting us up, but this time, we're afraid that our books might sully this beautiful house.

I had no real idea what to expect Athens to be like. Maybe I thought it was going to be a little more rock and roll. But really, it's just another college town with great herds of college kids doing what they do: partying, chugging beer, and shagging.

The reading in Athens was organized by Doug, a local poet, and he comes with us when we depart for Asheville, North Carolina, the next day. We stop at a Cracker Barrel, which is another magical place to me because in the late eighties, during the heydays of Queer Nation, the Southern and Midwestern chapters of QN had done an action against Cracker Barrel for firing a gay waiter. Cracker Barrel is a restaurant and Southern gift shop—i.e., homey tchotchkas with that suburban country kitchen feel, pastel rabbits and ducks, dried vegetation, and aprons and dish towels that either tell a story or have an elaborate recipe for some kind of pie. Their pork chops are great.

In South Carolina, half the billboards are of a Christian nature. Church battling against church for the souls and offerings of the believers. "Oh look, that's so sweet," Beth says as she spies some headstones on someone's front lawn. Until we drive closer, then we see that the headstones do not commemorate the family's dearly departed. Instead, they proclaim ABORTION KILLS in bright red letters. Later we will see trucks that have these headstones mounted on their beds.

We get into Asheville, which is supposed to be a liberal bastion of this part of the country. Whatever. Our hosts put us up at the local boardinghouse; apparently, the only boardinghouse. Beth and Doug end up in the girls' room since the boys' room is all full. At the reading later that night, we feel kind of weird that everyone seems to read their work as if it were Shakespeare-in-the-Bar. We seem so common and uncouth with our regular voices.

We nip back to Athens the next day, where we go our separate ways; Beth continues on to New York, and I hop on a bus to go to Atlanta. I've decided to stay at a youth hostel. Maybe I'm getting older, but it's getting harder for me to stay at youth hostels. The beds really hurt, and my bones and muscles ache like fuck. But there's something to be said for sleeping in a room with five other strange men, all in our underwear. Maybe it's me but I keep thinking that someone is masturbating and that I should be awake for it. I do not get much sleep.

In Atlanta, I end up at the CNN Studio tour seeing how they schlep their twenty-four-hour news show together. The tour guides look ragged, and they must be, having to schlep groups every other hour through the building, and saying the same vaguely informative lines and punch lines over and over again. But that's the nature of CNN. The same news programs and the same news reports repeat endlessly through the day. I especially love how the tour guides refer to their boss as "Ted" (e.g., "Oh no, Ted doesn't want to acquire any more satellites."), as if they personally knew Ted Turner, and as if he sat to lunch with them weekly to tell them his plans.

The news anchors—those bastions of hair, makeup, truth, and reliability that creep into our televisions nightly, or rather every single damn minute of the day in CNN's case—look really odd. Because of the studio lighting, they have to pile on that makeup, and in the absence of the television screen, they just look so phony. Typically, I would never trust anyone with so much makeup on their faces that they look like waxworks. There was supposed to be a Chinese-speaking tour, but because of the lack of Chinese-speaking tourists, the guides have dumped a Chinese family with this group without the aid of any translation. The poor family look lost and bored but like the newsmaking they're witnessing; the guides simply just don't care. The tour ends, where else, but in the gift shop, where you can buy all sorts of Ted Turner cable-station products: from *WrestleMania* and NWO Wrestling souvenirs to TNT movie memorabilia. Or you can get photos of yourself taken with a cardboard cutout of a CNN anchor.

Then it's off to the World of Coca-Cola, a three-story building that is essentially an advertisement for Coke. I've always liked Coke, it has been my preferred soft drink since I was a wee lad. The World of Coca-Cola shows us how Coke was invented and marketed from its beginnings all the way up to now. The best part of the tour was watching all those Coca-Cola TV ads from the 1970s to the present. I distinctly remember how we always looked forward to them when they came on the television, because they were just so catchy and fun and well made. Before you leave the building, there is a room of soda fountains where you can sample Coca-Cola products from around the world. It's amazing how some Americans have never heard of, seen, or tasted a lychee before. By the end of the World of Coca-Cola experience, I never wanted a Diet Pepsi more in my life.

I was fine throughout all of the South, but in Atlanta, suddenly the accents started to get to me and I just could not understand what the fuck a lot of people were saying. At the food court, I couldn't figure out if the guy at the Captain Cajun was speaking with an accent or if he was trying to speak Chinese to me.

Eventually, I make it home to San Francisco, home with all the freaks and weirdos and multi-culti pockets that make me love this city so much. Like all road trips, there is always a sense of leaving something of oneself and coming back with a heightened sense of it. I am glad I made this trip. Sometimes, we let our fear of the unknown and our preconceptions of a place prevent us from going where we please. When I told people I was going to do this trip, more than a few were shocked and asked why I was going. Wasn't I afraid of the racism and the potential for trouble? I, too, had a smudge of this fear, but as I traveled through the South, crossing state line after state line, and in and out of hundreds of cities where hundreds and thousands of people live and work, that apprehension faded quickly. Committing sodomy across four state lines did help make the trip a little more fun, too.

There are millions of lives out there, and each of them comes with its own stories and circumstances. I often hear reports of incidents of racism, homophobia, and gay-bashing in these areas, and I do not doubt that they do happen. But these also happen in the big cities. Perhaps we want to believe that the other, the people who live on the other side of the tracks, are more uncouth and less civil than we are, that they are capable of worse things.

If anything, this trip gave me a sense of connectedness with the country that I had never felt before. In some strange way, because of the way people opened themselves to us, I felt that I could belong to any part of this country. That I had a right to be there, and others would see that, too. That things weren't really all that different, just moving at a different speed. And I had never felt more American than at this time.

One of the best times I ever had on the road was when Justin and I traveled through the American south after the publication of our first Manic D books *Bite Hard* and *Monkey Girl*. We were in our twenties and going to cities we'd both never been before. My first thought was that this was going to be so much fun. FUN. I loved fun! Justin was hilarious to hang out with, so observant and snarky, and we were going to bro down with people we'd met at the National Poetry Slam. The only potential problem I could imagine was that I might drink too much beer and not be able to drive us to our next stop. At no point in the planning of the trip did the fact that he was gay, Asian, HIV+, or full of tattoos ring any warning bells. Spoken like a true white middle-class gal from the suburbs! What was there to worry about? We're all just people, right?

Reading this piece again, almost twenty years after our trip, I am struck by how much was going on for Justin as we zipped along America's interstates, stopping into small motels and gas stations and diners (and Graceland!), reading our poems to people in bars and cafes at night. His frenetic writer's brain was processing soap opera plots and celebrity gossip, Asian identity, American identity, queer identity, religion, iconography, violence, capitalism, and of course, pork and sex. My brain was like a cartoon dog in comparison, but Justin was happy to meet me where I was at. Once we were out on the road, I could see the wariness people had about him at first glance. We talked about it a little, but Justin was nothing if not preternaturally charming. He easily reeled people in with his sexy voice, his elegance, and his etiquette. Audiences would draw toward him and then he would slay with his anger and humor and truth-telling. Sounds so much simpler than it actually is. I would have remembered if anyone threatened or heckled him. And honestly, if you know Justin, he would have taken the first opportunity to mine any extreme drama that happened for this essay. Let it be known that the America we encountered together absolutely adored Justin Chin.

Justin's writer friends recognized his clearly enviable ability to fuse dark truths and unpleasantness with humor; to lay down something taboo and chase it with a dirty joke or some pop culture reference he knew way too much about. He could write a mean one-two punch that took you from something heavy to something funny (and by funny, I mean it could be gross, dark, weird, or stupid, or all of these at once). You'd be laughing, and it felt so good because a small part of you was still stuck in his hard truths. Relief, you would think, and then he'd go and pull another one.

There was a moment on our trip that was kind of like that. Shocking, dirty, distressing, funny. We pulled off at a rest stop to go to the bathroom. It was early evening in central Arkansas, not dark yet but getting there. I ran in for a quick pee and was back in the pickup in no time. Justin was taking forever. I started to worry. I realized I should probably go in and make sure he was okay. We'd been lucky so far, but who knows who you're going to meet in the men's bathroom at a rest stop in the middle of nowhere? Oh, wait. Justin knew. Justin had a pretty good idea who he might meet in the men's bathroom at a rest stop in the middle of nowhere. Not well-versed in the gay arts, I felt protective. I gave it a few more minutes and hopped out of the truck just as Justin was exiting the bathroom. I walked up to him and stopped, and he walked right past me, giving a quick nod. I kept going to the water fountain and turned around to see him sitting there in the cab waiting for me.

"Is everything okay?" I said when I got back in.

"If you sit here a minute, you'll see him."

And indeed some middle-aged white dad in khaki shorts and a polo walked out of the bathroom and got into a stationwagon with a woman in the front and two kids in the back. In the middle of nowhere. Off the 40. In Arkansas. Wife and kids.

"No!" I screamed. "No!!! You're kidding!!! Really?!"

"Oh, Beth. I love you," he said in that gorgeous husky voice. "But you're so naive for being such a slut!"

Undetectable

The space pod shrunk to microscopic
proportions with its inhabitants aboard,
injected in the vein of the terminally
ill coma patient. Traveling in the
bloodstream, we peek into the human body:
tissue, cell, organ, blood, lymph.
Every lucid hue taken away
by the black and white television set.
The mission: to reach the tumor,
to blast it with the specially designed
and shrunk laser gun. There are
complications of course, (why should
fiction not have a smudge of horrible reality?),
and Raquel, plucky scientist in her daring
skintight curve-enhancing wetsuit, swims
in blood to do something heroic,
but she is attacked by white blood cells, (eek!),
envisioned by the special effects department
as crunchy foam fingers, not unlike
the white fungus delicacy of soups
in Chinatown restaurants; deed
done, more white cells attacking,
oh how will they escape? Through the eye!

Cure or Blight. Who is
the foreign body here?

There is a battle in my body. Every day
a small chunk of me is given up in this
microscopic war. Small flecks of cells,
shreds of tissue, muscle, skin, bone
disintegrate, turn to junk, float
through my body and are pissed out.

This atom, this molecule, this bond
between them will quell the virus.
Squash it into almost nothingness,

into something so small, smaller
than it already is, so it won't show,
cannot be counted,
like ghosts and gases, its true existence
undiscovered, lurking
ready to kiss or kill. Undetectable.

Only in B-movies:
foreign body kills foreign body,
chemicals and petri dishes don't lie,
easy redemption, happy ending.

Everyday, a small bit
of myself dies
in that chemical battle.
      An undetectable bit
of myself dies everyday.

I get tired easily. I take more naps.
I dream less.
I smell like the medicine chest.
Some days I think I can
feel every single cell in me.
I can feel every single one
that dies.

Poison

Four men carry one,
each holding a limb,
wife trailing crying:
bit by a scorpion;

the evil culprit,
black in a jam jar,
rattles against glass.

Poison in the blood,
no feeling in arms and legs.

On the surgical table,
my father strategically
inserts seven fine
needles, newly acquired
acupuncture skills from Taiwan.

Soon, the man walks shakily,
slight limp out of the clinic.

Maybe there was more,
I'm sure there was more
to it than that,
but an eight-year-old boy
in pajamas and slippers
killing time
in his parents' workplace,

discovers that

    (and it marks him
    for the rest of his life)

there is a cure
for poison in the blood

put there by scorpions,
snakes, spiders, centipedes
and demons.

       And for a while,
the fatal, cancerous
world that spins
towards hell and destruction
slows its revolution,

and there is more
      day and more night.

Magnified

My brother got a microscope for his twelfth birthday,
hope of the family, excelling in all subjects, graced
with straight A's and a brain for chess, the gift
was an early enticement into the illustrious world
of medicine; but he was too busy playing football
to bother with it, so after it lay in its box
for months, I took it on as my own. Dinky, plastic
thing it was, but I felt like a scientist in a foreign
TV movie. I set the instrument up in our study room,
used the table lamp and shone its harsh bulb onto the reflective
mirror, redirecting the light through
the slide and into the magnifying eyepiece. The microscope
set came with ready-made slides: a tiny piece
of pink feather, a sliver of an unnamed insect's wing.
But I wanted to see what I wanted to see. I learned
how to prepare slides. I took a sewing needle
to the spore bags underneath fern fronds and scrapped
spores onto slides. (I saw round black saucers.)
I stripped leaves and petals of their epidermis
by painting them with Cutex nail varnish and carefully
peeling that layer of hardened goop off. (I saw
brick walls of cells in perfect order to respire and
to photosynthesize.) I looked at onion skins. (I saw
exquisite paperthins.) I looked at droplets of swamp water.
(But I saw nothing.) I caught ants — the small black ones
and the ferocious Kerringa fire ants — and pinned them
under glass slides. Still alive, their segmented bodies
struggling, magnified to horror movie proportions.
The red ants snapped their pincers in despair and anger,
the black ones waved their six legs in tired resignation.
Once I turned the magnification too high and the lens
crunched into the slide, cracking the cover slip, squishing
the ant. Its grizzly death, full of juice and torn
segmented bits, magnified 200x. I looked at moths' wings
and butterflies' wings, mosquitoes' proboscises, beetles'
legs. I looked at hair, saliva, dead skin peeled off from a sunburn, dried
blood from scabs, toenails, a drop of blood.

Later, my dad let me use his microscope. An impressive
thing: heavy and metal, not the light plastic toy I had
been playing with. And the magnifications were much higher.
This was how adults saw things. And everything I had seen
magnified before, was remagnified into a grander scale.
Cells broke into smaller cells, colors broke into a myriad
of more color and detail, light into more light. Amazements
into marvels, marvels into epics. The droplets of swamp
water that revealed nothing before now teamed with wriggling
things and strange life. The drop of blood now took on
more red, and life's movement shivered within that smear
on the slide. I looked at my semen and saw sperm cells,
the little bits of me wiggling their tails, swishing away
to a futile ruin. Everything I had dared to cram under
the lens and everything I could scrape and mount onto glass
slides was made up of small things of such delicacy,
and smaller things even, that when assembled
together constructed a greater beauty. The dead bits
lying on those slides were to face up to the harsh
realities of the world's atmosphere, to give flight,
to fight, to hunt, to repair, to prettify, to live as much
as the fragments, the living crumbs, held together.
And everything that was examined and dead, peeled
off and amputated, separated from its larger life,
was renewed with as much, even more
glory than the day, and the day after that, imagined.

One, the generously affectionate stray who stayed.

Two, the thug with the split ear and alley ways who tormented the first
one.

Three, the black and gray tabby with the crook in his tail that
straightened in his old age.

Four, the one now, the handsome one with the tail curl not unlike Kim
Novak's hairbun in *Vertigo*, who will talk to you, have whole
conversations even; for him the bed is the safest place he knows;
"something about saving each other."

And five, my white-socked mild-mannered friend, bookends to a third of
my life, where I was gung-ho and callow I grew into my doubt and
damage; who faithfully sat on the pillow by my head all those weeks
when I could not get out of bed; she placed her purr in the palm of
my hand. Those years, that summer, my heart knew its duty, it was
swathed in gray fur.

(Animal) Species I Have Eaten

Chicken, of course, and its liver, kidneys, gizzard, and intestines. I have also eaten its scaly feet but I do not care for them. Duck and its liver, and especially its crispy roasted skin. Goose and its liver. Quail. Sparrow (curried). Iguana (tastes like snake). Snake (specifically, python, tastes like squab). Pigeon (tastes like chicken). Kangaroo (tastes like duck). Alligator (tastes like pork). Horse (so I'm told). Dog (as meatballs). Rabbit (as stew, and as barbecue). Venison (as steak and as burger). Frog (legs and breasts). Turtle (in soup). Cow (call it beef, if you will, in all its blooded forms, and especially its stomach and intestinal lining). Lamb. Veal. Pig (call it pork if you want, and its stomach, intestinal lining, sexual organs, and lungs). Ox (tail). Goat (call it mutton if you must, some people object to its strong distinctive smell). Then there are the fish species: Haddock. Bream. Cod. Red Snapper. Grouper. Monkfish and its liver. Catfish. Stingray. Yellowtail. Salmon (and its cholesterol-high eggs). Tuna. Crab. Prawn. Crayfish. Lobster. Shark. Cuttlefish. Eel. Octopus. Squid.

There are also variations of unknown meats in sausages, Spam, deviled meats, corned beef, cold cuts, pizza toppings, ballpark hot dogs and roadside vendor wieners.

And then, there are eggs. The accounting of which has not yet been undertaken.

Giant Non-Poisonous Snake

It was neither its venom,

          for what could any of us know
          of its spit, its potency
          or deadliness, that it would hurt,
          sting, swell, but never kill humans,

nor its intent to attack,

          for it was content to sit
          in the dry drain warmed
          by the noon sun with its catch,
          a plump toad slow enough, unwitting
          enough, to be in the crab grass,

but its species, its ilk.
It was definitely its fangs,
and definitely its color,

          jet black scales worthy
          of an expensive evening handbag,

It was its slither and it was
that forked tongue that we could not see,
tucked underneath that petrified, slowly
digesting toad.

It was its reputation.

          Genesis. The Temptation.
          The forms the devil takes.
    "don't leave the cat's milk out overnight,
    it will attract cobras and other black snakes"

It had to be killed.

Two kettles are put on the stove:
Boiling water kills and disinfects.
    The first kettle's scald
would hurt, disorientate, weaken;
the second, if needed, if it could be poured,
since the snake would now be angrily lashing,
would weaken even more.
    Then the unrelenting blows from the bamboo canes

until the cord of black muscle lay lifeless.
The giant meat cleaver separates
the head from the body
in one hefty whack, an essential act,
                    who knows what sort of evil
                    will reanimate this dark thing,
                    this pawn of the devil.

The hewed head, jaws stretched
in ugly death, and its slack strained
body are picked up on the end of a cane
and tossed ten feet apart, back
into its grassy swamp home,
a warning to other snakes,
        poisonous or not.

The canes, defiled beyond saving, are wrapped
in layers of newspapers and thrown into the dustbin.
New canes will be bought from the market tomorrow.
The meat cleaver is soaked in boiling water for hours
to purge any hint of that evil blood.

And the spot of scalding and cleaving, stained
with spatter of thick dark blood blending into
the now powerless water, is doused
with bleach, and even more boiling water
and scrubbed, until
all traces of the clash,
                    the actual fear, of such protection,
evaporates, and the garden
and the home and its inhabitants
are restored to safety.

Juan Belmonte, matador, taunted the bulls he fought, *Me mata, me mata, toro*, as he had done since he was a boy, stealing into the ranchers' fields to fight them using his pants as his cape.

He was small and lame and bulls during his years as a matador gored him many times, but did not kill him. He did that himself when he was 70.

Kill me, kill me; Justin: the page, the stage; taunting it bare-assed or suited in lights.

The poem about "(Animal) Species I Have Eaten" is skinny. He told me he wanted to eat at least one of every animal of the air, the earth, the water. He'd just come from having eaten yak, and I forget what number it was, but he was short of 40 by just a couple.

The poem about the snake, "Giant Non-Poisonous Snake": he said once when he was a child his grandmother, at the foot of the stairs, told him in an angry voice to go back upstairs. He pretended to do it, but stopped and turned. There was a large black snake in the kitchen sink. He watched her kill it with a meat cleaver and a knife.

His inscription to me on the title page of *Bite Hard* reads: "Look what you've created Ms. Frankenstein." In one of the first chapters of *Burden of Ashes* he wrote of me, his then teacher, " 'No,' she said, 'this doesn't work, and this, and this. Fix it!' she exhorted. My heart felt like it had been poked with big sharp sticks... She was the first person to take my writing seriously enough not to humor me."

No flinching, no gabbling, no whining; a voice that scorches the pants off you; *damn*; how could I not take his writing seriously?

Grave

In the harsh glare of an easily
reprehensible life. The channel changer is lost
in the crack of an infinite sofa.
     Everything falls apart, everything breaks
down, torn into a million
          fragments, Jericho everyday.

I want to be the blameless
victim in this canceled puppet show,
the marionette every mother loves, the one
souvenirs are modeled from.

        (In that lifetime, Elton John will write mushy ballads just
        for me. Michael Jackson will want to be my best friend. He'd
        take me to Neverland Ranch, and by the llama feeding trough,
        he's say something like, "You're a great guy, don't give up,
        stay positive!" And I'd say, "Michael, you fucking idiot, I am
        positive." And he'd say, "Oh, you're so funny! Would you like
        to touch Bubbles?"
        And I would.)

In the crux of my hollow innocent youth,
I believed that my teddy bears had feelings.
     To cure me of this, my guardians made me give
them to the church missionaries' children.
Scrubbed-clean rosy-cheeked blonde kids who smelled
of sweat and talc, who were in constant
wide-blue-eyed bewilderment as to why
they were profusely perspiring in the tropics,
instead of living out some winter wonderland Bobsey Twins
fantasy, who were oblivious
to their parents' desperate efforts
to save the dusky masses, ignorant enough
to believe in the secret lives of stuffed animals.
        I could not eat animal crackers
because I did not want to hurt the poor things;
but, braised the right way, I could eat

any part of a pig, starting with the head,
working on the soft flesh around the eyes,
savoring its raspy tongue with a dipping
sauce of ginger, chilies and lime.

Oh blameless innocent victim.
What measures a lifetime?

I used to have this theory about how
much life a human body could hold.
It all had to do with the number
of heartbeats. Each human assigned a number
determined by an unknown power cascading
over the dark waters of the unformed Earth.

      For some, it was a magnificently high number,
seen only in Richie Rich comics, and for others,
it was frightfully low, like twenty-six.
          No bargaining, no coupons,
no White Flower Day sale, no specials. Once
you hit your number, you croak.
                I imagined the angels in heaven
and the demons in hell gathering to watch
the counters turn, like how I enjoyed watching
the speedometer line up to a row of similar
numbers, and especially when the row of
nines turned into
                the row of zeros.

Oh blameless innocent victim.
What measures eternity?

An eternal damnation. An everlasting love.

I could not imagine the night sky
stretched out forever, so I decided that it came
to an end at some point, by a velvet rope it ended
and beyond that rope were row after row of cushioned seats,
    a majestic cosmic theater,

playing every movie I can remember.

I want to be able to evoke
those blameless and innocent days, to revel
in their ignorance and goodness
as if they have the power
        to protect and to heal,
and to strengthen,
and to bring me to safety
        long after all other resources
                were exhausted.

But I emerge anew in the wreckage,
blinking in the sunlight,

the residue of salt water in my belly.

You know what they say,
God never closes a door before making sure
that the windows are barricaded
and the fire escape is inaccessible.

I used to know how to stop the revolution of planets.

I used to know how to save the world.

Now, I don't know anything anymore.

Harmless Medicine

The odds:

Chinese satellite spins out
of orbit and reenters the earth
atmosphere where it breaks
into twelve equal pieces; ten
chunks plunge into the Salton Sea
in a mad fizz; one piece, the tail,
hits a tin shack in a palm oil plantation
in Kelantan; the twelfth piece hits
you on the back of your head as you carry
a box of newly bloomed white narcissus bulbs.

———

At one time, they told me that the voices
in my head were the devil; at another time,
China; and another, the medications.

———

The water that pools at my feet in the shower:
amber, ochre against the white tub.

There are days when I think
it might be the chemicals leaching
out of my body;

or is it the soot of the city, the dust
and particles from the construction
behind my apartment, they're building
new expensive modern lofts,
I've left the windows open again;

or am I just dirty?

but this somber color:

as if I were washing orchid roots in the bath.

————

The leper rings his bell.

The leper bangs his gong.

The leper begs for alms.

The leper salves his sores with Tiger Balm.

The leper straps on a Stratocaster
    and tries to play a mean solo,
but his fingers snap off at the knuckles,
    like a jigsaw puzzle coming apart.

————

Ha Ha Ha Ha | Ha. Ho Ho Ho | Ho Ho. Hee | Hee Hee
Hee Hee. | Doo Doo Doo Doo | Doo. Tra La La | La La. ||

————

catheter:

blood flows in endless freeways
of arteries and vessels, exerts

a pressure, a force that drags

spiders into my veins.

————

Watching Manet's paint dry.

————

Alternatives:

The Gingko's not working.
The St. John's Wort I'm advised to avoid.
The Milk Thistle is for something else.
The Selenium makes me bloat.
The Ma Huang gives me palpitations.
The Multivitamins are good, but watch the Iron content.
The Echinachea does something weird.

The
    Gingko is.   Not.

Work.   Ing.

———

"...left this life, caught his last, left the stage, left us suddenly, passed away,
communes with the spirits, passed away peacefully, died peacefully, made his
journey home, suffers no longer, succumbed, passed peacefully from this life into
God's hands, soul left his body for his last eternal voyage, departed, left us..."

———

Insomnia intermezzo:
2:01 a.m.: documentary of ants mating
3:36 a.m.: machine that slices, dices, and makes life so easy
4:54 a.m.: looks like joan crawford in the twilight zone
5:15 a.m.: strange dream of canoeing in the sewer
7:32 a.m.: plane crash off the coast of southern california
8:01 a.m.: endless chatter, time for work

———

What is the taste of a tear
and how is it indistinguishable
from the taste of a thousand seas
of tears: a body of water so vast
and so salty, new life begins in it

everyday; and strange marine mammals
not seen even in the deepest plunge
of the earth's oceans live and thrive there.

———

The Proper Dosage:
2 tablets 3 times a day with a full glass of water.
1 capsule 2 times a day after a full meal.
2 tablets 8 hours apart on an empty stomach.
3 capsules 4 times a day with fruit juice.

The Problem:
If I leave San Francisco on a airplane at 9 a.m. traveling eastward en
route to Kuala Lumpur, and the plane crashes into the Himalayan
mountains, and I crawl out of the burning wreckage and find myself in
the mythical land of Shangri-La, where no one ever gets sick and no
one ever dies, calculate how many pills I should save from the flaming
cabin luggage, when I should take them, and what I should do about the
refills.

If at the same time, my evil doppelganger, the one responsible for feral
cat attacks on pharmacists, leaves Singapore at 8 a.m. and travels
westward, but with stopovers in Hong Kong, Karachi, Dubai, Abu
Dhabi, Copenhagen (cheap flight), and arrives at New York LaGuardia
in the middle of a snowstorm, determine what I should do about the
pain in my spine, and the adverse reactions to the prescribed antibiotics.

(please show your working calculations)

Bonus Point Question:
Calculate how many pills it takes to fill the Royal Albert Hall.

———

There's a trick I'm teaching my body to do,
to not mind the aches, the flu-like symptoms,
the slow brakes and creaking joints,
to ignore the nausea and the deathly fatigue.

I'm teaching my liver to love these toxins.
I'm teaching my heart to pump in regular 2/2.
I'm teaching my lungs to be swollen and greedy.
I'm teaching my stomach to do my belly good.

I'm teaching my blood to not mind the chaos.

———

Suture:

flesh to catgut kissed;

camouflage: scars,
indelicate pigmentation;

disguised as healing.

———

What wrecks us. What takes us
by the scruff and throws
us into the breakers, drags

us along the reef, drives
splinters into what's
left of our bodies.

What allows us to stand
this chaos in our veins.

———

Ignore the sky and all that is in it.
    Do not look at the ground

or where your feet are planted.
    What can it matter?

Trust where your body falls,
    the air it takes in,

the sweat of strangers,
    the ground it sleeps under.

———

Day starts as night.

And the evening and morning
were the next day.

Imagining America

1.

If the world has seen America through the movies,
I imagine how the world has seen me.

If America has seen my homeland through the movies,
I imagine how America has seen me.

The has-been actress on the telly plumps pity with a side of
    Christian do-good. Her red fingernails rest on the knobby
    head of a belly-bloated child,
even as the promises of the spilled semen of green cards & Amex
    holidays slash their way across the Third World.
Even as the gay community clamors to join the military,
a drag queen in Malaysia bleeds to death after a group of soldiers
    hacks off his penis to teach him a lesson.

                        "Take it like a man, boy."

Even as GIs & soldiers go on R&R in the sunny Third World,
    screwing their way into the psyche of a queen named Exotica,
a 16-year-old boy dies because of the infection caused by the sex toy
    that shatters in his rectum, shoved there by his Big Daddy who cries
    & moves on to the next one.

                        "Take it like a man, boy."

Even as AIDS inches further into wounds of the Third World,
the AIDS-infected flight attendant lives out the rest of his life
    in Bangkok, screwing without a condom & living out his dream
    of spreading his love to a bevy of beautiful boys.

                        "Take it like a man, boy."

Go ahead & plumb the Third World for your sense of spirituality,
    your fuck-me-all Godhead fix, rest easy in your futon feeling that
    you're making an affirmative gesture.
If you can't afford the sex tour, join the Peace Corps.

Even as the Land of Opportunity devours its poor, tired, hungry masses
    yearning to breathe free, we're asked to be silent, quiet, don't make
    waves, don't offend, do nothing, buy a new pair of sneakers, sit back
    & enjoy your favorite decaffeinated red, white & blue cola.

I'll take it like a man.
I'll take every inch of it like the man you want me to be, like the man
    I'll never be, like the man the world wants me to be, the man
    Asian-America wants me to be, the man my dog wants me to be.
Take it like I got a chip on my shoulder, —hey, what's your chip?—

If America has seen me through my cuisine,
I imagine how I would taste.
On the days when I've been the hero, the monster,
the slut, the piece of shit. Some other permutation of myself.

If I have seen myself through the movies,
I imagine how I have seen myself.

I'm tired of explaining how it feels.

2.
Foreigner, stranger:

        The hidden face of our identity.

        A border between human bodies
        patrolled by suspect, guarded

        by hounds trained to sniff
        out every inch of your body.

                Swimming past Kansas.

Native   tourist   other.

Citizen:

The foreigner is detested
because we refuse to recognize

the foreigner within

ourselves.

3.
Bruised sky scarred
with tissue shreds of clouds
guide the flying night insects bug-speed
into the windshield of the car.

Each greeting of abdominal fluids
become bats with outstretched
inviting arms, trash
on the road becomes roadkill

good enough to eat,
and the marshy grasslands, steep cliffs
that shear steeply, a skid mark
away into dark nothingness.

The redwoods wrap around the bends,
clinging to sickly fog,
the decreasing speed limits,
until the cricket silence pulls

us into a meandering calm.
Should we have stopped
at that last truck stop,
or that last motel with the free

cable and heated swimming pool?
Should we have stopped even at all?

Another roadside diner, and another
Grand Slam breakfast that tastes

of the same cheese, the same grease,
as every other on this tarmac circus.

The familiarity, the lack of surprises,
the same security of regular
unsurprising coffee in regulation white mugs,
filled with hot coffee that cools fast.

Night breaks into chilly
bluish dawn, the rain darts
on the glass windows. The first
trains rumble by, headlong

into the day and noon and fog
and still of our ever-changing country.

4. (Fleet Week, San Francisco.)
These are not angels,
for what angels are driven by men,
    and what angels spew
such smoke and pomp and earthly noise.

    Seven fighter jets,
the glint of afternoon sun
on their navy tails and wings, fly
        in V-formation: metal ducks
heading south to bellicose warmth;
a show of warring plumage, fluffed for
    an infinite wintry aggression.

    And on the ground,

children cling to mothers' pants
    in awe and wonderment, a streetperson
waves, certain dogs yap in utter

confusion, tourists and locals
    look up at the swooshing spectacle.

And on the ground,
an old Asian women drops
her shopping basket, throws herself
to the ground in a fetal ball,

   her wrinkled old arms wrapped
around her head, covering ears
and thin hair, waiting

         for that moment of impact.

But there is no
      sharp churn of shrapnel and earth and fire
on the ground.

She picks herself up off the pavement, her eyes
ignore those of an old Asian couple
who dashed for cover in a nearby doorway;

she gathers her basket from between two parked cars,
brushes herself off and rushes to the market;
a new truck of fresh chickens has just unloaded.

   No bombs dropped here today.

. All shelled out.

   Strategically deployed many years ago.

   But only some have started to detonate.

These angels are blue indeed.

5.
American dogs cannot eat chicken or tomatoes or they will die. If your
dog dies, you can be arrested & put in jail.

There is vegetarian lard, meatless sausage, turkey pork, wheat-free bread, non-dairy milk, & fat-free sugar.

Everyday, a new cereal, a new cola (diet & decaffeinated), a new chocolate bar, & a new shampoo are invented by scientists working in big factories.

For your health, there are vitamins from AA to ZZ, herbal extracts to supplement the vitamins, oxygen tablets to supplement the herbal extracts, bioenzyme capsules to supplement the oxygen tablets, powdered Chinese medicine to supplement the bioenzymes, yoga & pilates to help the Chinese medicine absorb properly, aerobics machines to help you get the most of the yoga & pilates, crystal healing to help center you after the aerobics, aromatherapy to take the edge off the crystals, & psychotherapy for all-round general health & well-being.

The ultimate plateau for any celebrity in America is to become a spokesperson for anorexia nervosa & bulimia. Celebrities also lend their winning personalities & star power to educating the public about a whole range of health concerns, social & political issues & making sure that American history & America's place in world history is not forgotten.

A tragedy is not considered tragic unless those involved appear on television on a newsmagazine show or a talk show to talk about their experiences. Similarly, no moral lessons can be truly learned unless it is revealed & pontificated upon on any number of national television callin shows.

Freedom of speech guarantees that everyone must have their say; everyone must talk & speak & voice their every opinion & thought; from newspapers, magazines, radio shows, talk shows, call-in shows, soapboxes, electronic mail, the internet, skywriting, & graffiti, there is no shortage of quiet space that cannot be filled with the talk & chatter of American twang.

Lawsuits are the new form of activism. To make a difference in the community, you must sue your way across the political stratosphere, spinning courts & jury trials & giant cash settlements & punitive damages.

The supreme American ideal & its most prized commodity is Truth. It must be taught in school, invoked in discourse, preached from pulpits, stenciled on nuclear missiles & used in all its godlike glory.

A survey conducted among American homes found that 87 percent of the nation believes that Red, White & Blue are the primary colors of both pigment & light.

6.
In the night of ten million stars,
each so distinct in their own space
in the heavens, along a long straight
road that passes from one desert town
into another; Palm Desert, Indio,
Indian Hills, La Quinta; strip
mall upon strip mall, filled
with the Lego blocks of Americana;
the gods of the American Dream
buy and sell, offer discounts,
markdowns, special leasing deals
just for us. Each, none more carnivorous
than the next; resorts and hotels more opulent,
more elaborate, and totally disconnected
with the environment than the next:
Egyptian culture, Rome in the desert.
On a long straight road, driving
at night, the street lamps dimmed or spread
so far apart that the patches of darkness
in between seem something like comfort;
the blanket that covers us when we sleep
so trusting and secure in our own beds
in a world we will never truly own.

7.
My memories are stained with the familiar.

They are not perfumed with silence.

The round-trip ticket is inscribed in my punch-wild mind.

No luggage to check.

I have wanted too much for too long.

Not a smudge of this dust belongs to you.

Nothing true promised.

I cry for your vanity.

I search for your tender.

I wake for your savage affections.

I itch for an impenetrable contract.

Body permutates into falsehood.

Every queer chip clearly in place.

I have known too little for too long.

Queer for home.

Splendid refuge.

Return.

8.
I imagine America.

I see a sea of coffins, smooth & polished, twisted of fragrant wood,
     filled with potpourri & the ashes of Bibles.
& in these coffins, a sea of waxy bodies overpoweringly quiet, as in life
     & in death, fighting none, defying none;
carrion for crows & vultures to pluck & feed, for countless virus
     & bacteria to regenerate.

It is said that those who die too early, too soon before their time,
will come back as the most powerful ghosts, presiding over their
houses, dominant to a crushing fault;
but for those who die on schedule, there is no such power but what the
living do for them. In this ever imagined America, there lies a
haunting battle of such love; a distillation of a thousand century
beauty.
And here is the body that bears the contract of false colors, the scrutiny
of day & of night, of milk & of salt.
Here is the body that aims for the highest familial constellation, the
lowest degree of tractability.
Confronted by the great mirror of this love, I come deep & dark &
queer.
Confronted by the great mirror of America, I come queenly & elegiac, I
come intractable & longing;
burden of grief & hardship, burden of irretrievable tonnage, the
fluctuating stuff of hearts & lives, I come perpetually reconciled;
bellyful; pissing in my wake an antidote to bitterness.
Subjectifying my returning want & flesh from non-creation; returning a
crest of invisible skin; this is how I breathe in the pages of space &
pictures & peculiarity;
I will not make a silent sound; I will not be numbed by the misfortunes
of the present.
These are the last days here; & every approach now free from suspicion,
brimful of every silent right, falls into place; desire, mine; breath.
This is my occurrence. This is the sound of my indisputable body.
The necessity of speaking; the antidote to every bitterness, to all that
ails, to imagining America in our waking dreams & in our childlike
slumber; to imagining America in what remains,
& that which is hidden, that which hides, that which is blind, that which
sees all, which is unseen, which is unspeakable, unmentionable,
which dares not speak, which is whispered, which is true, which is
lies, which is punished, which is taken away,
& that which is time, that which is laughed at, that which is mistaken,
that which is illness, that which is granted, which must be repaid,
which is free, which is freedom, which is years, which challenges,
which is challenged, which ends all, which births, which passes,
which angers, is shame,
is no more.

9.
All you refugee dreamers & crocodile wrestlers,
I'm fumbling to make you American.

Everything has been swept away.

I see a history called lifetime.
I see a lifetime burning down.
I see the death of the body.
I see the death of the nation.
I see the death of the family.
I see the death of memory.
I see the death of nostalgia
I see the death of borders.
I see the death of the sky.

I create my culture everyday.
I write a bible of diaspora.
I piss in the embrace of men.
I bruise the broken speech.
I lullaby the dead in fields of fever.

And what are you going to do?
And what will you do?

I say I will find a new place that is mine.
I say I will find some place,

I say, I say, I say.

I'm imagining America.
I'm fumbling to make this mine.

The Men's Restroom at the INS Building

Cold marble, remnants from the building's past
when its sturdy quake-proof foundations
remembered what it was like to have
the country as its invading founders intended;
now, handed down from one governmental
budget to another, it harbors
what the country wants to be.

The thick insulated walls and double doors
of the restroom on the second floor of
the Immigration and Naturalization Services building
effectively muffle the sounds outside
its portals, so that the occupants can do
what all humans must do at some point, even here.

Every time the door cranks open
on its creaky rusted hinges,
the outside filters in. Immigrants:
tired, poor, hungry, huddled;
energetic, well-off, well-fed, unhuddled;
All, submissive as cattle, humbly waiting
for the butcher, passively queued in neat lines,
waiting for forms to fill, waiting to pay
another bloated fee; checkbooks, cash, money orders
in hand, paying for the privilege to file
document after document, and endless streams
of paper, in duplicates and copies and certified copies,
to be processed, stamped, approved, temporarily
approved, an identity issued, a documentation
procured, a proof in hand.
Until the expiration date creeps around
too soon, and the cycle begins anew.

The marble walls of the toilet stall
are covered with graffiti, Sharpie black,
written in firm brazen hand.
    Tony was here.

el norte.
Roberto loves Suzie.
PIGS! DEATH TO THE PIGS!
INS officers are assholes...
Who the fuck are you to tell me I can't stay in the country
This is the only place in this cold
building where anyone in those endless
lines can regain a sense of significance,
to hold heads up. But this self-worth
is short-lived when the door creaks open,
and the militant bellow of the country
protecting its land from sea to shining sea
percolates in: the rumble
of language difficulties, bilingualism
defeated and failed, fear
and incomprehension taking over.

Here, in the restroom on the second floor
of the Immigration and Naturalization Services building
the air can be very still, but each time
the door opens, the roil of deferred hope
and amputated convictions is enough
to quake the foundations to bombed rubble.

Gutted

My favorite children's bedtime prayer
is the one that goes:

> Matthew, Mark, Luke and John,
> The bed be blest that I lie upon,
> Four angels to my bed,
> Four angels around my head,
> One to watch and one to pray,
> And two to bear my soul away.

This is such a vast improvement
over the more popular,

> Now I lay me down to sleep,
> I pray the Lord my soul to keep.
> If I should die before I wake,
> I pray the Lord my soul to take.

The difference is that
in one, you get to go
to bed with four men.

But in both, the child is afraid
he will die in the middle
of the night in his sleep.

> (Why? What's going on in these homes?
> Where's Child Protective Services when they're needed?)

Later, the child will grow up
and realize the lie hidden
in those prefabricated prayers.

That is what most people want:
to die in your sleep,
to die in your own bed.

Tonight, again

The sitting ghost is on attack again tonight.
He's twice as fitful, back again tonight.

When I wake from this, will I be a man or boy?
If this were *Flashdance*, we'd be hearing "Maniac" again tonight.

One hand plots murder, the other strains to understand.
The body's every sigh is sidetracked again tonight.

Call out the National Guard; evacuate the trolls to safe ground.
I'm matchbook & gasoline, I'm burning bridges in stacks again tonight.

Greyhound, rabbit, pony, racehorse, NASCAR, motocross.
Hope take one more fluttering spin on the racetrack again tonight.

Those limp wrists beget such limp applause.
There'll be no encore for the egomaniac again tonight.

I gave the conductor my fare, I've got my transfer.
I'm ready to climb on board the wagon again tonight.

I'm slipping down the barrel of this pigpen.
Looks like it's bareback again tonight.

The things that give you pleasure are someday going to hurt you.
Are you ready to flail & fail and take some flak again tonight?

Under all the sand in the Sahara, all the fossils melting into oil.
How can these bones lay down their arms afield again tonight?

All these flags, rotting red white & blue on cars, walls & poles.
These are personal wounds, flown to staunch the ache again tonight.

Under all the clodded dirt of mass graves & cemeteries,
When can these bones rest in arms unweary & appeased again tonight?

In the peaceable kingdom, the lion & the lamb may lie together.
But on earth, their each own lies aren't worth a quack again tonight.

In grieving, how frightfully far is the sea to shining sea.
Every day's every incomplete mourning affects again tonight.

We pray so that God knows He exists.
Who should be blamed for His lack again tonight?

Dexammethazone, cyclopamine, vincristine, rebetol, interferon, temodar.
Acyclovir, stemastil, neutrophil, tamoxifan, teslac again tonight.

What's next, what's next, and then, and then.
Blah blah blah, over and over, again and again, again tonight.

A liturgy of how we fell; a list of obstacles that trip.
O Litterbugs! Is all this payback a gain tonight?

I'm never quite as good as when I bleed.
I won't deny the hypochondriac again tonight.

Burgundy for sex, Bordeaux for intellect.
The wino looks for a corkscrew in the haystack again tonight.

The heart's blackmarket trades in things unknown to us.
Here's my left-ass, may I have another whack again tonight?

Crucify or complain, but the needle's found the vein.
Tell me, while we're waiting, all the drawbacks again tonight.

The exile describes, remembers, then imagines.
His dreaming interrupted by flashbacks again tonight.

We invest all our cracked eggs into one omelet.
How much interest did Mr. Banker gain tonight?

Riding the mule to look for the White Horse.
Guess who's the insomniac again tonight?

I pulled the cord, signaled the driver to slow down, to stop.
I want to get off the wagon, find my tracks again tonight.

What are the limits of one's grief, of what one creature can bear?
Who will witness how it eats your heart as a snack again tonight?

When the road map doesn't continue on E16, Pg. 45 nothing.
Strong lifelines on such tiny hands: I predict a wreck again tonight.

My spectacular failures, my holy spooks, my brilliant bugaboos.
Hold on, little boy, you're going to bruise like heck again tonight.

Gutted used to be my favorite book by Justin, and then *98 Wounds* happened. Justin's latest book was always my favorite, partly because I was so hungry, always, for his particular brand of tragedy and absurdity, decay and sweetness, nightmares and pop culture. The way Justin brought it all in, everything, the whole gamut of life and its clashing crashing attendant emotions – it was as if the entire human experience, rendered shamelessly, fearlessly, honestly, comically, was available to you. A complete complicated world of feelings.

It had been a while since I'd picked up *Gutted*, and the first poem, "Tonight, again," destroyed me. Its simple, raw force, its undercurrent of compassion, of self-compassion, the poet showing the poet tenderness for he knows his weaknesses, knows the stakes of them, and is about to go there anyway.

The grind of the poem feels like a body memory. What is the narrator after: dangerous sex, the heady obliteration of wine, of drugs? It's all in there, pick your poison, pick all of them. The choice to knowingly indulge your compulsion, the longing not just for pleasure or oblivion but wreckage, too. A litany of pharmaceuticals appears among the vices, reminding us that Justin had a relationship with chemicals, with his body's need and mortality, that surpassed simple addiction. He lived as long as he did thanks to chemicals; he wrote about it often.

Reading "Tonight, again," I imagined Justin as the little boy in the poem's last line, making a final, affirming peace with his *spectacular failures . . .holy spooks . . brilliant bugaboos*. We watched in grief and fear as another one of our own took that solo journey into death. I hope there is another side; I hope I find him there someday, again.

I would not mind getting the cancer
that Ali MacGraw gets in *Love Story*,
the cancer where as you lay dying,
you become more beautiful and more moisturized.

The classic death would be Garbo's Camille,
but all that coughing and flopping around on the bed
is just so undignified. I realize she had consumption,
but at least Nicole Kidman in *Moulin Rouge*
still managed to karaoke with her consumption.

I certainly wouldn't want the cancer
Debra Winger gets in *Terms of Endearment*.
"Come to Laugh, Come to Cry, Come to Care, Come to Terms."
Oh, just go away already.

The death I would most like
is Bette Midler's in *The Rose*.
Where, up on stage in front of a packed house,
I'll tell the story of the first time I heard
the blues, and as the story winds down,
my speech all slurry and raised to an odd minor chord,
I'll wonder, Why is it so dark? Who turned off all the lights? Where has
everybody gone?
                              Then I will collapse and die.[1]

My one request for my funeral
is that at no point should "I Believe I Can Fly"
be sung, played, hummed, mumbled, muttered,
mentioned or thought of.
                    This is how poltergeist activity gets started.

But I know, I know my death
                    will not kill me.
Rather it is the death of others
                    that will kill me.

[1]While the strains of "The Rose" play in the background. I want the version that is a duet with Bette Midler and Wynonna Judd. That is the gayest rendition ever. Before you even get to the second verse, before you find out that the one who won't be taken cannot seem to give or that love is only for the lucky and the strong, you just want to be fucked up the arse.

For those of us who came to terms with being queer during the AIDS years, Justin was a beacon of light—well, a somewhat strange light, a beckoning beacon of fucked-up light: Come unto me, all ye that labor and are heavy laden, and I will give you not rest exactly, but the burden-lifting sigh when someone gets you. Come onto me, all you queers, you freaks, homos, all you night crawlers, you weirdos, dwellers of the margins, and I'll show you what's up.

At a time when most of the writing that was supposed to reflect our lives was maudlin claptrap, Justin's poetry polished the rust off my heart. The world we lived in was crazy; he reflected that, not some sentimentalized image of it. No last trips to Paris, no post-funeral packing of fabulous sweaters in suitcases given by parents who lived in the old country of Oklahoma, no angels descending from Heaven to witness a saintly lover's final words. When we were overwhelmed with grief that should not have been borne by anyone, he refused to soil his acerbic tongue with trite.

James Baldwin once wrote, "Sentimentality, the ostentatious parading of excessive and spurious emotion, is the mark of dishonesty . . . the wet eyes of the sentimentalist betray his aversion to experience, his fear of life, his arid heart." I don't know if Justin had a fear of life, but if he did, he was so over it. And he certainly had no aversion to experience, any experience.

In his poems, he referenced high and low art, he mixed the mundane with the sublime, the arcane with argot, because it was how he experienced life. But it was also how he was able to break through a reader's defenses.

In this poem, excerpted from *Gutted*, he opens with the sappiest of all images, Ali MacGraw's death scene from *Love Story*, which isn't just lowbrow art, it's the lowest of the low, no one can limbo that. Granted a reader should be wary—I mean, just a tiny bit, you know, Justin is talking about the big D, but really, Ali MacGraw? Let's make fun of her. And then he gets cheesier—I mean, Greta and Nicole and karaoke? That's just silly. And funny. No, not *Terms of Endearment*, don't go there, Justin. He does. He builds up to the corniest movie death scene yet, Bette Midler in *The Rose*. Yikes. He certainly has his pop culture down. R. Kelly, anyone? And then, in the gut, the sucker punch.

How can a reader prepare for that?

I wasn't prepared for his absence.

(Happiness)

When it first appeared on the scene
all across Old Europe, it was used
to wish luck upon,
as if, and is it not?
based on an outlaw's luck.
Except for the Welsh
who traded luck for smarts.
           Did wisdom beget happy
           or is it happier to be wise?
It took half a century
before it absorbed gladness.
Given life expectancies at that time,
so many of the lucky and the wise died
not knowing the giggles.
But still, it took another 190 years
before its condition was recorded.
And another 406 years before it
was extended to clams.
Prior to that, clams and other bivalves
were nothing if not sullen and tasty.

           Waking with the one you love.
           The sleeping and purring cat in bed.
           Wonderment shared with little nieces and nephews.
           A good prayer. A good book.
           A meal with friends.
           A day without care or bother.
           Remission.

Happiness is never overrated.

The other night, I dreamt of a father who lasted forever.

I loved him and I loathed him. I scorned his gifts.
I disdained him and I wanted him.
I wanted him to see me, yet I lurked in the dark.
I respected him and feared him.
I saw his gold, I saw his shit, I sold his gold and shoveled his shit.
I stole his shirts, his car, his fillings.
He caned me, belted me; I was naughty, a disciplined child.
I broke his bones, and then his spirit. I fed him and clothed him.
I held him to my breath.
He was comfort to my terror, I lived in such mighty abandoning waves.
He soothed my homesickness; he was my home, I his sick.
I counted his pills, prepared his shot. He did not complain. I bitched like
    mad.
He never shed a single tear, even as I filled rooms with mine.
I slept fetal by his side, dreamt his dreams.
I stoned his dreams. Oh what mighty boulders I flung at his pebbly dreams.
He gave me all the food that money could buy.
He gave me an ulcer no money in the world would look at.
I made him presents of my youthful blame, such lovely bitter nuggets.
I obeyed him and I trusted him. He saw to it that I always did.
I showed him the rose that had bloomed in the garden and he showed me
the hole where we could bury the cat.
I understood his ways. I prayed with him, for him, around him. And
when he wasn't looking, I prayed for someone else.
He took the chip-shot off my shoulder, I took the chips out of his old
    block.
He hid my ugly scars and I built us a house of cards, all aces, sevens,
    & jokers.
I shook the dust off his wings, hoping he would fly and show me how; he
took the sleep out of my heart.
This time I would be the one who went away, the one everyone counted on
who didn't stay.

In this dream of the father that lasted forever,
my dad forgave me, and this time, I learned to forgive myself.

My rage then ceased to need a name.

A dream only becomes one
       when you wake up.

I wake up.
I am lying in rubble.
Everything is mud.
My homes have become holes.
I have no strength to sit up.
I have no shovel.

The four leather golf bags, wrapped up in white plastic trashbags against the dust and sun, hang their shrouded club heavy heads like skulking nuns in the corner.

When awoken sweating from the heat in the middle of the night during a revolving brown-out, they might be hooded mynahs mourning in the company of monks.

Two days after my dad's funeral,
I am playing with my three-year-old niece.
She has just kicked me out of the tea party,
exiled to the sofa to observe only,
no pretend finger foods for Uncle.
Mid-party, she picks up her Elmo cell-phone.
"Hello," I hear her say into the bright red mouthpiece,
"No, Kong-kong is not at home now; he's in heaven,
okay, goodbye." She stops and considers for a while,
then she allows me back into the tea party.
But only if I take sensible bites of the fish sandwiches
she has prepared, and sensible sips from the little teacup.

That I can do.

Me and My Helper Monkey

It has come to this at last. My health is on the blink,
and I am informed that I cannot qualify for all the super
home health services my city offers. But do I really want
the volunteer from the health agency, some stranger working off
his multitude of parking tickets while squaring out his karma?
Who's got time or push to strap down the stereo, hide all valuables
and imported beer, the good CDs and books?
                                                    No, what I really want
is simply, a helper monkey. A gamely gibbon, or a plucky baboon.
Even an agreeable howler monkey. But most of all, a nice fuzzy
spider monkey. Certainly not chimpanzees, they're too focused on
their showbiz careers to care about anyone else. And certainly not
Orangutans or Gorillas, because they shed like fuckers
and are constantly doped up on dried coconut husks. No. I shall
have a lovely Spider Monkey with a wizened beard, preferably,
and I shall call my helper monkey, Steve.

Oh what grand times Steve, My Helper Monkey, and I will have.
His chores are to retrieve the mail from the down the stairs,
scoop the cat poop and change the cat litter, wash the dishes,
collect my laundry from the wash-and-fold, buy Diet Coke
and Ben & Jerry's from the corner grocery, and return my DVDs
to the local neighborhood video store. With Steve, My Helper Monkey,
I will no longer suffer any nonsense from the surly clerks
at the video store. No more will they over-deduct credits
from my card, charge me nonexistent late fees and accidentally lose
the 10-rental credit I paid for. With one screeching fang-baring snarl
and its ensuing spray of saliva possibly tainted with Ebola, Steve,
My Helper Monkey, will make things right again at that Evil Hole.
I will make Steve, My Helper Monkey, a small coin pouch that he wears
strapped across his monkey chest like a Prada shoulder bag.
He will be the envy of all the other helper monkeys; lesser monkeys
with their Kaiser fanny packs cannot even bear to look at him.

I will remind Steve, My Helper Monkey, not to swing so carefree
from the phone wires. Reminding him of one particular monkey
I once knew long ago in my childhood. That little monkey was named

Foo, and he belonged to my neighbor, the loud-mouthed, wife-beating,
Doberman-rearing lawyer Joseph Aw. Foo was such a delightful
little monkey. Every morning, while the Dobermans were eating
their vittles, he would swing on over to our kitchen window
and just hang there. Mom would feed him small cut-up pieces of fruit.
Even my stern dad was won; "so bloody cute," Dad clucked,
and gave him a piece of buttered toast topped with a generous lump
of orange marmalade. Foo was a happy monkey, swinging around
the neighborhood, being fed by his legion of admirers, talking
to the macaws in the trees, singing happy songs with family dogs
and cats. But one day, the poor thing was swinging on the phone wires
and he made a connection, positive to negative. It was a hotline
1-800-Collect Call to the Monkey God, who accepted the charges.
Poor Foo was burned to a little crispy thing. His body was stuck
to the phone wire and as much as Mrs. Aw tried to knock it down,
first using a long pole, then eventually, by throwing sneakers at it,
the charred body stayed stuck to the phone wires and so she left it.
Foo hung on to those wires for months, a memorial to his loving
carefree monkey days, until his body decomposed and fell off.
His body fell off but his arms still clung to the phone wire
like notes on a music score, a sharp note held on by a cracking jazz
musician. Eventually, those flea-infested arms that would hold you
so lovingly around your neck decomposed and fell off too; now all
that was left were his fingers, mere knuckles stuck to the wire.
Steve, My Helper Monkey looks at me, his monkey eyes fearfully wide
and quivering with tears; in his high-pitched monkey screech,
he promises that he will be careful.

With Steve, My Helper Monkey, in my life, I can finally go
to Rainbow Grocery to buy bulk rice. At the prices they charge,
you would think they would get one of the stoned hippie employees
to park his damn bicycle, and come inside to help pick the weevils out
of the grain. That is all moot, now that I have Steve, My Helper Monkey,
with me. With his nimble fingers, and his blood memory of picking nits
whilst grooming assorted siblings and cousins, sorting the weevils
out of a sack of rice is no problem. We do this chore together,
spreading the sack's contents out on the kitchen table. Steve moves
fast, and more than occasionally, I have to stop and chastise him
when he can't resist eating the crunchy weevils so packed

with beta-proteins. "Spit it out!" I scold, holding my palm out
and Steve, My Helper Monkey, sheepishly pulls out the weevil
he has put into his mouth. I know it is hard for any monkey to resist
this fat protein snack, but these aren't weevils you find in a forest,
these are vegan co-op grocery weevils, who know what carcinogens
or cooties they harbor. Sometimes I pretend to look the other way;
sometimes, Steve, My Helper Monkey, is just too fast, slamming
the weevils into his mouth and chewing them down before I notice.
Inevitably, Steve, My Helper Monkey, comes to me a day or two later,
looking all piteous pointing to his mouth. A weevil is stuck
between his teeth. "Serves you right!" I scold again, but he and I
both know that I will eventually floss his teeth for him.
While sorting rice, Steve, My Helper Monkey, and I realize our bond,
we realize how truly alone we are in this world. My family
and homeland so far away and I somewhat disconnected from them;
and he, his jungle razed to the ground so the 12th largest
football stadium in the world could be built; where in the off-season,
Rainforest Benefit concerts are held, featuring Sting who assembles
a group of malnourished underprivileged Amazonian Indians as his
back-up singers. Steve, My Helper Monkey, is amazed
how the natives managed to work their lip-plates around
the difficult consonants of all those annoying Police songs.
He was so sure those lip-plates would come dislodged during "Roxanne."

Every day when the weather is good, Steve, My Helper Monkey, and I
go for little walks in the neighborhood. He swings merrily from
lamppost to treetop to traffic sign above me. Cute boys with dogs will
stop to check us out and give me their phone numbers. Life with Steve,
My Helper Monkey, is not all hunky-dory lovely walkies. One time walking,
we passed the Pier One Imports. And something snapped:
Steve, My Helper Monkey, suddenly went berserk, as if a primal force
had possessed him. He whipped off his new Kate Spade backpack,
and dashed into the store, howling and heading straight for the Fall
wicker collection. He climbed into each and every wicker basket
and hamper on display, crying and snarling and smearing handfuls
of his feces all over the wicker coasters, lampshades, and placemats.
It was awful. But none more than the time I discovered strange oily
smears on my flatbed scanner. Then wiry dry hairs stuck
to my computer keyboard. Steve, My Helper Monkey, was having

an Internet affair with Julie, a helper monkey in Wisconsin,
who was assigned to a young woman with MS. Late at night,
Steve, My Helper Monkey, would scan dirty dirty pictures
of his glowing monkey ass in heat and e-mail them to Julie.
I had to let the affair run its course. I know the pain of love,
and I know the greater pain of not loving. Then,
Julie's guardian was miraculously healed by Pastor Benny Hinn
on his evangelical tour of the Great Lakes. Julie was gone.
Just like that. Poor Steve. How he pined. So much so that he lay
on the futon, unable to move or groom or scratch, struggling to breathe
and to make sense of life and love in all its baffling permutations.
The roles were then reversed. It was I who had to care for him.
In his weakened state, in what we all thought might be his final
night, Steve, My Helper Monkey, reaches for the Palm Pilot
with his prehensile tail and slowing types a message to me. *Steve.*
Want. Ba Na. He is too weak to continue but our bond has become such
that I know exactly what he wants.

                              I bake him Banana Nut Bread
topped with a thick cream cheese frosting and a generous sprinkling of weevils.
                              Like all broken hearts, even monkey ones,
Steve, My Helper Monkey's heart mends and we return to our daily grind
and grinding, we resume our little lives so filled with trifles
and cheers; until the turning of that day when my health
irrevocably fails. Here in my final days, Steve, My Helper Monkey
performs his grandest gestures. He knows it is my vain and miscarried
dream, my secret desire, to grow into being the sort of man
who can get away with a name like Scooter, T-Bone, Boomer or Clifford.
In my dying moments, Steve My Helper Monkey takes the Epson Label Maker,
which he bought online at Overstock.com, he just could not resist
the free shipping, no monkey can, and he types those names out
one by one, in every font and size, on every last label.
He gently sticks each label, one by one, to my fevered forehead.
Then, perplexed as to why my body is so cold and stiff, he swings over
to The Gap and shoplifts a woolly sweater which he tries to put on me.
But rigor mortis makes that a difficult task, even for such a clever
monkey, so at my wake, Steve, My Helper Monkey, attentively sits
by my coffin and makes sure the sweater is draped over me at all times.
He is confused, hysterical when I am shoved into the crematorium,
and desperately grabs hold of my foot to stop me from sliding

into the flames. But the heat and the gas burners singe his fur
and he lets the foot go and runs off into the trees screaming
holy terror, anguished that he didn't hold on tighter
or with all five limbs.

At my grave, Steve, My Helper Monkey, sits
on my headstone waiting for me to come back, and go rice-sorting
with him, to help him download monkey porn. Like Greyfriars Bobby,
Steve, My Helper Monkey, sits on my headstone diligently waiting.
Well-wishers bring him small plates of food, which he nibbles from,
but he never leaves his spot. Nothing would make him move from that
one spot, not rainstorms nor hail, not drive-bys nor parades;
mating seasons come and go and his monkey ass glows red then back
to brown until it stops glowing altogether. The back of my headstone
is streaked with syrupy monkey pee, and positively covered
in monkey poo. Still, Steve, My Helper Monkey, waits. Until
one Spring day, 17 years later, overcome with exhaustion and old-age
and sadness, Steve, My Helper Monkey, looks up into the trees
and in the highest branches, he sees me sitting with Julie,
I'm holding a Tupperware bursting with banana nut bread, frosted
with cream cheese and weevils. Steve, My Helper Monkey, sighs, quietly
screeches his monkey screech, then he tips over and dies.

He is buried in a plot a few feet away from me.
A small monument is erected in honor of my helper monkey.
His coin pouch is bronzed. Every year, thousands of seeing-eye dogs
and helper monkeys make the pilgrimage to his grave. They pee
and rub their hindquarters against the marble monument
to my dear helper monkey.

And in a jungle somewhere so deep
that no one has yet discovered, a tree grows, a new species
whose flowers blossom and produce a fruit that tastes not unlike
banana nut bread frosted with cream cheese. Weevils are naturally
drawn to that fruit. A whole wilderness of monkeys live in that tree,
not realizing that in those fruit lies the miracle serum
that can cure all human illness.

Justin was well known for his mordant quips, but he could be sweet too, and one would sometimes theorize that he had been hurt in love early on and developed this carapace of satirical humor to protect himself, like Idina Menzel's Elsa in *Frozen*. In the back of my mind I can hear Justin wincing that I am comparing him to a Disney cartoon character—but Justin, she is one of the obsessional ones! And you loved your Disney too, didn't you? I know one case at least.

"Me and My Helper Monkey" unrolls the hard surface to reveal the tender side within, and that comes as such a relief in the saga of his father's death that makes up the bulk of *Gutted*. We all know the syndrome of caring in which someone else's problems loom larger than one's own, until the moment death disappears them, and then after a single beat, one remembers one has one's own problems. It's at this juncture in the story of *Gutted* that we hear of the adorable Steve, "perplexed as to why my body is so cold and stiff." Like Greyfriars Bobby, the Skye terrier at the heart of the crumby 1961 live-action Disney programmer of the same name, the faithful pet won't leave his master's grave, for love has reasons even death can't refute.

Grief comes in waves,
high tide, low tide, till it's done.
Time harbors, sets its breakers and fail-safes
but grief comes in such waves;
set adrift, eyeshot far from tomb and grave
still, the floods flash ash to ashes to dust
Grief comes in lapping waves
high tide, low tide, never done.

Narrowing

Less than a month after they tore down the freeway overpass, disused since the earthquake, they're tearing down the projects across the street with cranes and wrecking balls, earthmoving equipment; all sorts of heavy iron machinery boom, making the entire building shake, the windows rattle and hum, the panes vibrate like tuning forks in all their termite-cracked minor flats; they've unleashed something into the air, those old buildings are like sporebags, crack them and next you know, things are growing out of stuff, and voila! you have sourdough and some sort of yeasty new beer, but my respiratory passages can't bear this new air much more, I've tried over-the-counters and two different prescription inhalers and still, it's all snot and tissues, drips and a tissue, laboriously breathing through the mouth, which will only lead to a sinus infection; pity, it's so nice out, spring weather in the middle of fall, and I want to go look for some discarded drawers at the secondhand thrift store; I like that aesthetic though at times I feel the pangs of wanting and needing more grown-up furniture, but how can anyone pass up the drama of a thrift store, a place so rife with heartbreak, where the remnants of a past era of living – stuff that was once the newest of the latest, the must-own fad, the pride and joy of a home – find refuge; in primary school, we were assigned English compositions where we had to write the 'autobiography' of an inanimate object, like a pen or a kite or a pair of shoes, and I don't remember any of the heroes of those accounts ever ending up in a thrift store; I can see the one regret of not living a long time is the amusement of walking into a thrift store at a point in the future, to see it filled to the rafters (or will they have done away with rafters by then?) with all the Philippe Starck and Alessi crap, bottle openers made to look like toadstools, chairs made to seat gray alien butts, all that hyper-designed stuff all for under a buck; but the fatigue is getting the better of me, my options are to fight and not let it get the upper hand, because once you're left with the lower hand, you'll be forever sifting dirt, or I can just give in graciously, the breathing situation is not helping and the days are getting shorter ever so progressively, but what that really means is daylight shortens, days are always twenty-four hours, but that's moot, since I don't have quite as many good hours in a day as I once had; just as the daylight shortens, as day shortens, so life narrows, which I never in my wildest thought it would; as a young man starting out in the world, I expected life to expand in roiling curlicues, like how gases fill a space or how smoke talks to clouds, but our 'ways' set in, comfort levels peak, tastes and preferences solidify, tolerance and curiosity harden, each decision made or deferred shuts down more doors than I knew even existed, bit by bit, the six-lane highway leads to a single rural lane, a cow walking this gauntlet would wonder if it leads to a branding, a feed trough or the abattoir, sometimes, it might even lead to a grassy meadow but the cow doesn't know or expect that; the building stops rumbling and quaking as if in awe of the encroaching sunset; sometimes, usually during the good hours of my day, I understand that there are those who take a certain joy in this narrowing.

Lately I've been thinking
about the longstanding nature
of love and of happiness and all that stuff.
About my life as it stands
held together with little bits of string.

In my early life, my need to belong
and my need for security made me accept
such stupid and lethal conditions.
   In my later life, I should have known
better but the stupid and lethal stuff
was always the most fun.

When I was of that age, I thought
the question coming was to be:
      "What have I done with my life?"
      "How will I be remembered?"

Now, that I am at the age, I realize
the question should have been, and was always:
      "What have I done to my life?"
      "How will I be forgotten?"

"How would you like to die?" he asks.

"How anyone would," I say. "In my sleep, in my own bed." I could turn the question around back to him but the answer was, if not obvious, then at least suspended in our air. So I say instead, "How would you not like to die? What's the worst death?"

"Anything involving lava, or quicksand," he says.

"Is there still quicksand? Didn't the U.N. and the World Health Organization eradicate that in the late '60s?"

"No, they gave up after polio and smallpox," he says. "Your worst death?"

"Animals," I say. "Being eaten by some wild hungry animal. What would be really awful is if the animal had a small jaw, and so it has to take lots of little bites to finish you off."

"On the flip side of that, can you imagine being mauled by panda bears?" he says. "Wouldn't that be the cutest death ever?"

"Or else," I offer, "a headline in the newspapers might read: Autopsy reveals that man killed by three-toed sloth actually died of late stage cancer."

A week ago, we watched a TV movie on cable called *Strays*. A family – father, mother, young child, and newly born infant – moves into their dream home out in the woodsy suburbs. And then the nightmare begins. They are stalked by a colony of feral cats. The alpha male cat, the principal evil who's supposedly afraid of water (obviously), looked like he had been dipped in a bucket of K-Y Jelly and barely towel dried. The tag line for the movie was *Cats have nine lives, you only have one*. There was a lot of clawing and scratching and more clawing until their victims inexplicably died. And not to mention with inflamed sinuses, too. I believe one victim even threw himself off the third floor balcony to his death just so the awful mewing and clawing would stop.

It's a cliché in horror movies when, during a suspenseful moment, a cat would suddenly fly, or rather be flung, screeching and meowing across the screen. In this movie, however, that tired ruse made perfect sense and it happened quite frequently as well.

"What's the collective noun for cats?" he asks.

"A bunch of cats? A furby of cats? A plié of cats? An allergy of cats?" I say guessing, but he's already dozed off. Then, now, it's darkening in gradual sheets outside and in here, and he's getting tired. When I leave, I will go to his apartment and attempt to tidy up, put things away, pack things up.

What more can I do? Twelve days ago he left for his medical specialist's appointment and never came back, sent straight to hospice care, and his apartment is evidence of that. Everything – every object and piece of furniture, every wall hanging and scrap of paper, every appliance and implement, every book and record, every withering houseplant and all the pillows on the bed, even the air aswirl with particles of dust and dander – hangs as if in mid-sentence. It's a kind of heartbreak I never knew I could or would ever recognize.

It is mid-day, an ordinary unsurprising type of mild any day, when I get a text message from him which reads *This is kind of it, kiddies. I'm feeling one fry short of the Happiest Meal. I feel like I'm underwater more and more each hour. Thank you for everything. You are all precious to me.*

A whole lot of cats is a clowder, a clutter, a cluster, a colony, a glorying, a pounce, a kindle, a litter, a dout, a parliament, a seraglio, a glaring, a destruction.

But here I shall make a break: Let the young ones be queer the way they want to be queer, as long as they are queer, as long as they find among themselves each other to love. I've given up the dream of the Queer Nation. Race, class, gender, ideologies, and values will always divide us. It is ludicrous to think that since we share a common passion, we should all want the same things out of this life. We are each other's angels, and we are each other's demons. Beyond ourselves, there will always be those that wish for nothing more than to see us dead: They have been wishing and acting on it for centuries, but we are not vanishing. Call it sheer luck, call it divine intervention, call it tenacity.

Ask any good Chinese family. The pecking order of desirable professions is: Doctor (neurosurgeon or cardiac surgeon is best; failing a career in medicine, dentistry is an acceptable runner-up). Lawyer. Engineer. More liberal families would probably accept Accountant, and possibly an MBA from an American Ivy League university. If you are artistic, you are expected to be an architect.

These professions confer upon the practitioner's parents bragging rights of the highest order, and these rights are used to great effect in smiting down kith and kin. A well-timed brag in the battlegrounds of golf courses and aquarobics can transform others into bitter green-eyed monsters and substantially elevate one's standing in society.

Writing is just not done. Sure, it is done, but by the children of poor, sad parents who have to forgo all their bragging rights, sitting tight-lipped at family dinners and (Horrors!) class reunions, where they have to endure scads of pity and scorn. If any writing is ever done, it is done For Fun, and possibly to win essay contests so that, again, the parents can rub it into the faces of relatives who have lesser idiot children.

This was Singapore in the '80s. Enough time had passed since the country had gained its independence—first from British colonial rule then the Japanese occupation and then from the collective peninsula of Malaya—for the children born of parents from the riotous days of the shaky, race-conscious '60s to be making their mark on the Great Society. Their parents had given them an independent country-state, and now it was time for them to make good on those droning When We Were Your Age lectures their parents launched into at every opportunity.

Academics were the equalizing factor among races and social classes. Do well in subjects that mattered, which were the sciences and the maths, and boyo, you were in. Everybody admired you. People saw in you hope, redemption, and Great Things. The kids, brought up in this atmosphere, were very much coconspirators in this whole scheme. Visions of mansions in the twisty-winding roads of chichi Commonwealth Avenue or bungalows in Bukit Timah hills and trendy lunches at the most prestigious country clubs danced in their eyes.

At home, we had tuition for as many subjects as were deemed needed. After school, some poor hapless graduate who could not get a real job would come to our house and give us extra lessons in math, Chinese, and the sciences. Parents bought assessment books that textbook companies churned out by the baleful. These were workbooks filled with difficult math sums, baffling chemistry equations, and physics problems, all with the correct answers in the back of the book. Many of these very same questions had once appeared in state final examinations, so they were the real thing. Rumour had it that they might appear again in any given year. So parents, teachers, and children all furiously worked these into the fabric of their lives.

There were English assessment books, full of grammar exercises designed to help one learn tenses, vocabulary, sentence construction, punctuation, and all those idiomatic things to do with the English language. There were even English Composition books, in which the publishers would print examples of exemplary compositions, all written in crisp, perfectly constructed English sentences. No run-ons, no complex sentence structures, no postmodern meanderings, just perfect little clause-phrase or phrase-clause sentences, with one exclamation point thrown in somewhere to give it a spark of life. Some of my classmates at school memorized a whole bank of these compositions so they could regurgitate them at examination time, scribbling them down from memory, word for word. We were given sample answers for our English literature classes so we could give correct answers to Shakespeare, Achebe, and *The Crucible*. There was a correct way to write, to think creatively, and to be creative. In Secondary One, the penultimate year of our general education, when we still had art class, a classmate of mine even enrolled in art tuition, where his art tutor made him practice the same two drawings all semester so he would ace that final art exam and bring his grade points up even more.

The act of writing was not held in high esteem. It was seen as something wholly self-indulgent and a complete waste of time—time that could be better spent figuring out how to be a neurosurgeon. In a country where the press, the theatre, the cinema, and practically all artistic expression was closely monitored by the government, writing was also an act that could conceivably get you into real trouble. It seemed like a hoary temptation to actually speak one's mind, to say something against the grain, to challenge authority.

The parents lived through the creation of the National Security Act. They witnessed Communists, Communist sympathizers, opposition party leaders, and people who were vocally critical of the government being arrested and detained without trial. The detainees had every shred of their reputation excoriated in the local government papers and were jailed for

God knows how long. "Better not say anything, better not make waves," parents warned their children. "Much better you go study and become a doctor. Make loads of money. After all, in the end, it's money that talks." Writing did not promise wealth of any sort.

There were local writers and local playwrights, but they were looked on as "the artistic crowd": effeminate poofters, bored housewives, and people with real jobs who wrote as a hobby. These were people who entertained with their talent but did not contribute in any meaningful way to the Scheme of Great Things that was happening in the country.

Occasionally there would be a blip on the screen. A play would be closed down, a book banned, an occasional playwright or writer questioned by the government for certain themes in their work.

Once, a playwright was commended for his play about the plight of Filipino maids in Singapore. The play received raves in the papers when it debuted at the local arts festival. Two years later, that very same play got the poor bloke in trouble when the government found out he was acquainted with some people who may have had communist leanings. The play was held up as an example of subversive communist propaganda trying to fan the flames of class issues in the country. Much more recently, members of a local theatre company were hauled in for questioning and their company's rights to perform yanked after it was discovered that some members of the group had attended Augusta Boal's Theatre of the Oppressed Workshop in New York City. *How did the government know?* some wondered but did not ask publicly. But in the end, everyone knew that the government just knew things.

But most of the time the writers accepted their lot in this repression. They grumbled, they griped, and they dreamed of the freedoms of the West and of writing that scathing yet witty novel, an indictment on the government and society, which would win the Booker Prize; but then the touring company of *Cats* trundled into town, and everyone would be licking their whiskers, practicing their rendition of "Memories" at karaoke bars, and clawing for a place in the furball chorus.

Other writers simply stayed far away from the line, churning out quaint little local-flavoured comedies. True crime, detective stories, ghost stories, and romance novels were the most popular books published and read. There were a number of local novelists whose works were not terribly well read or taken seriously. Fiction and poetry and writing and novels seemed like such a Western thing, all those words and ideas. And certainly these piddly local efforts could not measure up to the canon of British literature that was the

God-sent cloudstack leading us out of our native wilderness, could it now?

I enjoyed reading more than anything else. I read at a level higher than my grade, starting with Enid Blyton books and then Agatha Christie mysteries by the time I was in Primary Three. I enjoyed these fantasy worlds, these other realities, these stories.

Inspired by our reading, a friend and I excitedly tried our hand at writing our own little stories. Somehow, the other kids in the class managed to recreate these fabulous stories and get them printed in the school annual. Now, 20 years later, I suspect that their parents helped them. But then, even as I was proud of my piddly little achievements, it crushed me to realize that my 9-year-old mind could not keep up with all these other minds around me. Worse than that, my mother found the very first story that I had written tucked away in my school bag. It was a twee, plotless, illustrated-with-coloured-pencils thing: Some spaceguy gets captured by aliens, blasts them with a laser gun, and escapes. But I had trouble with the proper usage of "than" and "then." My mom was livid. Besides wasting my time on such a worthless nonacademic activity, how could I also not know such a simple thing? Severely scolded and that evening's television viewing privileges yanked, I was made to write 20 sentences, each using "then" and "than" correctly. My first stab at writing a story ended up in tears.

After that I hid my fondness for writing in my English composition classes rather than be berated and put down for my "hobby." (Yes, like stamp collecting and comic books, that was the only thing it was allowed to be. My parents tried to persuade me to switch to chess; it was a much better hobby since it used the brain, they argued.) I tore into my composition assignments like mad, writing essays and narratives. All through my school years, while my classmates hated to write these compositions once a week, I was secretly delighted to do them. It was the only thing I was good at. I had been sent to the science sequence and I was not doing too well in school. I had above-average grades, but that wasn't going to be good enough to get me into medical school, was it? Nothing but straight A's was expected.

My father was one of the first in his side of the family to go to university: medical school, and on scholarship no less. It was no small feat. My granddad, the jolly old bigamist, was a butcher (we always had the best cuts of pork). He had 12 children and two wives to support, so money was tight. Accomplishment and success were important things to the family. Dad met Mom when he was a resident working off his scholarship obligations. She was the night nurse on the ward. (I'm glad I wasn't a patient on that ward;

presumably not much hospitaling was done while the night nurse and the night doctor were making goo-goo eyes at each other and plotting to go to the Rose Show on the weekend.) Mom had come to the nursing profession by defying her father—good girls from good families became teachers, not nurses swabbing at syphilitic sores and changing geriatrics' bedpans.

When your parents are both in the medical profession, everyone and the cat simply assumes that you will be too. Sitting in the back of my dad's clinic, patients often asked when my brother and I were going to take over our dad's practice—and this was when we were still in primary school. The notion of taking over the family business is a very Chinese thing. And when the family business is something as prestigious as medicine, the stakes are raised.

Among my school chums, the ones whose fathers or mothers were doctors all knew they were to follow suit. One school chum's father pulled every string, calling in favours from friends on the board of directors and the chair of the Old Boys' Association so that his daughter, who had never ever taken a science class in her school life, could rectify her shameful mistake and be enrolled in the science sequence. She flunked horribly.

In an effort to make me study more, I was forbidden to read any books that were not curriculum-related. Anytime I was caught reading a non-textbook, I was scolded. For a few years, I even gave up reading altogether.

Then one day a few years later I discovered an old book of my late uncle's. It was *The Collected Works of Oscar Wilde*. The fat tome with its funny, sad fairy tales, weird and beautiful stories, rekindled my love for reading. I started borrowing books from the school library and the British Council library. I wandered among the bookstores looking at the books I could not afford to buy, but took note of their names so I could find them in the libraries.

I hid my reading: I read on the school bus and after everyone had gone to bed. Occasionally, my grandmother, shuffling to the toilet late at night, would stick her head into my room, catch me lying in bed with a book, and nag me for "not studying" and threaten to tell my parents.

Reading also refueled my wanting to write. So, once a week, I looked at the assignment on the blackboard and delved into that oh-so-frivolous act of writing. It could have been an argumentative essay or those assignments requiring the student to finish a narrative, given the first few lines. I wrote feverishly and happily, my pen pressed into the ruled notebook, until my fingers were cramped; it was a feeling I loved, how those digits ached and how the muscles hurt as I pulled my fingers back to crack my knuckles in order to relieve the pressure. My grades for my compositions were nothing exceptional, but in the dreary hours of school it was the most enjoyment I got from any class.

I did not think that I wanted to be a writer. I wanted to be an actor. I had acted in a school play, a multicultural production of *The Diary of Anne Frank* in which the Franks and the Van Daams were Chinese, Muslim, and Indian, and I was hooked. I had done this without my parents' knowledge, and by the time they found out it was too late to yank me out of it. The play did well; it was one of three plays selected to be part of that year's Arts Festival Fringe.

I wanted a life in the theatre. If my parents had known, they would have been horrified. Already my mom had cautioned me about people in "the theatre." She warned me that a lot of them were "funny."

"You mean, like, comedic?" I replied, feigning innocence.

"No… homosexual!" she whispered. If only she knew I had been having sex with men ever since I was 13 years old, and maybe all little queers find their way to the Drama Club one way or another.

I started hanging around the people in the local theatre scene. It was the first time that I socialized with other gay people. It was nice having gay friends and confidants. I had avoided the queens at school because I did not want any of the teasing and bullying they endured to be redirected toward me. Hanging out with these out theatre fags helped me overcome my own hang-ups. I started to be comfortable around even the screamingest queens.

Young pup that I was, I did not yet realize that a whole constellation of worlds has always existed within already existing worlds. But here and now I came to that epiphany. In this microworld, playwrights and writers were revered, and I wanted the kind of adoration and power they wielded. Inspired by all my readings and from watching stage productions, I thought that I too could write something fabulous, perhaps a truly subversive account of gay life in Singapore in the late '80s, which would also serve as an indictment against the government and society. I would be the toast of The Scene, profiled in the Arts Section of the *Straits Times*, where Dinesh D'Souza, the lispy, flaming theatre critic and rumoured porno maven who preferred little Noorlinah Muhammad's overenunciated performance as Anne in *The Diary of Anne Frank* to my stately, multifaceted brooding Peter, would be amazed by my brilliance. Wouldn't that show my folks what was what?

I withdrew money from my savings account, dashed down to the Yaohan electronics department and bought a typewriter (which I still have to this day), and took my first shaky baby steps toward writing. I was a Day-Glo existentialist (hey, it was the '80s), writing purple prose and utterly overblown pretentious poetry about death, ennui, and the ickiness of Life: *The seed of Eve spat from my mouth / lies barren in the futile soil!* Fueled by pop music, I descended further into the ungodly realm of Hallmark schmaltz. I was fast headed for the saccharine swampland ruled by Susan Poliz Schultz.

After royally fucking up my A-level examinations, I came to the United States to take another stab at an education. Here I quickly learned that I was a bad actor. More horrifying, I was a bad ethnic actor. I had this strange accent, I was completely untrained, and I was completely uncomfortable in my body. I realized quickly that I was never any good and that my landing the role in that school production had less to do with talent than with the limited number of boys who joined the Drama Club and weren't screaming flaming queens who wanted to wear wigs, dresses, and ply on the Max Factor. I also knew that I would not get any good, no matter how much I tried. It was just not in me, and besides I could not bring myself to take acting classes. Yikes, that would be frivolous! Self-indulgent! A waste of time! Wrong! My socialization had run deep grooves into me.

In my first semester at an American college, I felt I had to pick major and so I chose journalism. It seemed like a practical choice and it combined the best of both worlds: what I enjoyed doing and the prospects of getting a Real Job.

At Hawaii Pacific College, where they accepted anyone with a pulse, I enrolled in my first-year English class. One of the assignments was to do some creative work. The lecturer held up my work to the class as an example of "powerful" and "emotional" writing. In actuality, it was just plain bad; it was the poetic equivalent of the power ballad—all syrup, manipulation, and easy payback. Ms. Fischel enjoyed Chippendales, Michael Bolton, and Kenny G: I should have known better. But I was pleased and held my head high among my classmates. After that semester, I transferred to the University of Hawaii, and in my first semester there I sorted through the schedule and signed up for a writing class. By some sheer stroke of luck, I ended up meeting Faye Kicknosway. She was a tough broad, weird in that Midwest writer sort of way and quite intense.

Sitting in her cramped, sunny little office by a bookshelf towering with little chapbooks and small press treasures, she scribbled comments and red-lined my poems. "No," she said, "this doesn't work, and this, and this. Fix it!" she exhorted. My heart felt like it had been poked with big sharp sticks and I wanted to cry. She was brutal. I pulled out the big guns, those poems from the previous semester that Ms. Fischel had loved. Faye glanced at them, looked me straight in the eye with a horrified look on her face, and said, "No, don't ever do that ever again." She was the first person to take my writing seriously enough to not humour me.

It was enough to make anyone want to throw in the pen wipes. But one day I turned in two pieces and, to my surprise, she loved them. She offered suggestions on how to edit and shape them. Her upper-level class was going to do a reading, and she invited me to read with them. When I showed up at the dry run of the reading, I was nervous and intimidated. But it was also the turning point of my life: Little did I know, that day would be the start of my life as a writer. At the rehearsal there were two writers who wowed me. One was a sassy local woman who wrote these poems in the voice of a tita, and the other was this young, well-groomed, fey Filipino guy with big, sculpted hair who wrote these hilarious poems about his mother and about cruising the men's bathrooms at Sinclair library. During the break the two of them came up to me, arm in arm, and said how much they loved my work. They were Lois-Ann Yamanaka and R. Zamora (Zack) Linmark. We talked, and Lois-Ann invited me to join their writing workshop.

Soon, every Sunday afternoon Lisa Asagi—another of Faye's students— and Zack would pick me up and we would drive to Kalihi to Lois-Ann's house. We whipped out our poems and read our work to one another, and then proceeded to workshop what we'd written. We recommended books to one another, bought books for one another, and lent one another books. We stalked Jessica Hagedorn when she came to Hawaii. Armed with the *International Directory of Small Presses and Little Magazines* and ragged copies of *Poets and Writers*, we encouraged one another to send out work to various journals and presses. We comforted and kvetched when we were rejected, rejoiced and feigned jealousy when someone was published and the others not. We all wrote very differently but we understood one another's voices and processes and aesthetics.

Lisa, Zack, and I also hung out a lot on the weekends, drinking heavily (Lisa, conveniently, worked at the Liquor Collection at Ward Warehouse) and going clubbing. Lying on the floor in Zack's Waikiki apartment, we wrote poems and stories chronicling our obsessive love interests, our screwed-up romantic and familial relationships, our mad wild lives. We were queer for Anaïs Nin (but we now know better—that she was just a slut with a diary), Lorca, García Márquez, Barthes, Genet, Winterson, Jane Bowles. We shared our writing with one another at every opportunity, we inspired and goaded one another to create new work, we supported one another unequivocally, and we developed a language of our own that allowed us to turn the stuff of our queer little lives into something real on the page.

With Lisa, Zack, Lois-Ann, and Faye, we never second-guessed that we were anything but writers. It was that tits to the wind abandon that gave me the permission to believe that it was okay to be a writer, and that I was one. That writing wasn't something frivolous and vain.

I visited San Francisco in the summer of 1990. I went to as many readings as I could. I saw Diane DiPrima, Sharon Olds, Galway Kinnell, Robert Hass, Allen Ginsberg, Judy Grahn, and a bunch of obscure poets at Small Press Traffic whose names I have forgotten. Every Thursday night I went to Cafe Babar for their open readings. The corrugated tin walls and the secondhand-smoky air reverberated with an exhilarating intensity. Poets were heckled with unrestrained candor and applauded with genuine admiration and respect. Of course, in all the weeks that I went there I never had the nerve to read my work. I returned to Hawaii in the fall filled with what I had witnessed in San Francisco. The street poetry and all its verve, the people who flocked to literary readings, the used bookstores chock-full of treasures—Small Press Traffic's shelves brimmed over with these little books, each one painstakingly put together by someone not unlike myself. It all showed me a world of possibilities that until then I never knew existed.

On Christmas Day 1990, Lisa and Zack drove me to the airport and I boarded a plane for San Francisco. Away from the gang, doubt set in. But the seeds had been planted and they had taken root, and I was still terribly driven to write and to send my work out for publication.

I did not ever think I could be a writer. I did not think I had anything worth saying. As the youngest child in the family, my opinions were always taken lightly, ridiculed, or ignored. My parents believed in me: They believed that I could be anything they wanted me to be. I kept my writing hidden from my parents for a long time. I knew they would think it was a distraction from the highway leading to my degree and my real job. Even after graduating from college, I still could not tell them. I did not think that I could not bear their criticism and scorn, their carefully executed frowns designed to instill maximum shame. I just could not bear to have them sully this one thing of mine in any way.

R. Zamora Linmark published *Rolling the R's*, a highly acclaimed debut novel, went to Manila on a Fulbright Scholarship, and is finishing his new novel. Lois-Ann Yamanaka has published a number of books to a certain amount of acclaim and controversy, and was recently featured on the cover of *Poets and Writers* magazine. Lisa has published stories in various journals and we are all looking forward to her first novel, if she ever gets her shit together to finish it.

Borders opened a brand-spanking-new 24-hour store in the middle of Singapore's tourist district: It has a bistro and café and is so busy that the clerks can only restock the shelves from midnight to 6 A.M.

I met up with a friend of mine when I was last home. Her dad and my dad were classmates in medical school. "Tell me about your book," she said to me over coffee. "Your mom is so proud of you, and she keeps telling my mom all about what you've been up to in the States. And all the books you've done." I'm always the last to know. Then again, I wonder what she really said.

Now my mom calls occasionally and cautions me not to write anything bad about the government or anything at all about the family, especially her. She sends me little clippings from the back of magazines, of classified ads that promise thousands of dollars of prize money in their "Poetry Contests." "Why don't you try to enter, you're good at writing, you can make some money!" she cheerfully suggests. I try to explain to her that these things are often scams. But in her mind the idea of creative writing, of parlaying my ephemeral talent into cold hard cash seems like such a sure thing.

Recently the Malaysian police arrested two people for what they had written in their emails. In the throes of the country's failing economy, the two had dared suggest that there was a smidgen of racial tension in the land. They were charged with "gossip mongering" and were detained without trial for two years in order to "preserve national security."

In my life, writing has been and still is something that is dangerous, politically and privately. The act of writing occupies a limboland. It is necessary but feared. It is a brave, albeit foolish act. Even writing these pages fills me with a certain dread. Growing up in an atmosphere of censorship and repression, where one generation who learns to keep silent and play safe passes those fears on to the next generation and the next, takes its toll; it does what it's supposed to do. Writing is an ongoing risk. And it is a risk that I take on, maybe because I know no better way to make sense of this mud of life. Every day I have to fight my feelings that what I do is trivial, frivolous, and meaningless. And in the end, in the dustbin of my history, when all is decaying and rotted, composting to bits, whether my work survives after me, or even survives the next few years, will remain to be seen. What I know is what this work did: It gave me the courage to speak, and to find some semblance of myself worth the words. And that act has in no small way loosened the straps on that old muzzle made in the government store and sent to every home and every parent who willingly, or perhaps not so willingly, put it on themselves and their children, and their children after that.

Everything has been swept away.

I see a history called lifetime.
   I see a lifetime burning down.
      I see the death of the body.
         I see the death of the nation.
   I see the death of the family.
    I see the death of memory.
      I see the death of nostalgia.
        I see the death of borders.
          I see the death of the sky.

       I create my culture everyday.
     I write a bible of diaspora.
   I bruise in broken speech.

And what are you gonna do?

      I say I will find a new place that is mine.
    I say I will find some place
I say, I say,

I say.

Faggot Dinosaur

The faggot dinosaur sits on his haunches and surveys his handiwork,
writ across the walls of his cave lit by stone lamps.
In iron oxide and clay, in verdigris and moss,
in mulch and meal, the scene is as luminous as a fevered dawn
dream, fervid as a wild memory.

The migration of the wooly mammoths.
The mating feasts of the horned water buffaloes.
The balls-out struggle of the amphibious.
The peaceful truce of the vertebrates

The faggot dinosaur is pleased.
The deep reds he gets from those creatures by the salt-lick,
which he painstakingly masticates into a workable pulp,
if he pulls the bones out before hand, he discovers
the reds take on an altogether different hue:
an opalescent lava, then a neon sunset.
The umbers and ochres everybody knows
you got to get knee deep in the mud-flats and dig
deep to get the best stuff, and for the still
incomplete blue notes, he'll have to wait till the end
of summer to get that, for when those bulbous fruit growing
by the primordial swamp ripen. Not yet there,
he checked a few days ago, it'll be months more,
but who knows when really.

Everyone's buzzing about the electrical storms,
the scuttlebutt is the flaming asteroid storm barreling
towards the earth and sea. The faggot dinosaur pays
scant attention to the yammering crowds. They've never
been right and he's never been interested in all
their useless twitter.

By the swamp, he finds a new clutch
of those soft-shelled creatures trying to walk on their two hind limbs.
So adorable. So utterly delicious.
And he likes to eat them on toothpicks.

But all the other dinosaurs laugh and ridicule him for it,
foux-la-la, they mock, as they devour their prey in messy chomps.

The taunts matter little to the faggot dinosaur
but for one brutish rex, who he's too shy
to even look in the googly eye.
Oh, I would never poke fun at your short little arms, he thinks.
No, I would groom the spots you can't reach. Every last spot.

But tongue tied, the faggot dinosaur retreats to his opus.
The final touch will be the silhouette of two dinosaurs
watching the world before them evolve.
But he'll need a pile of blue for that. He'll be patient.
It's not like I'm going anywhere soon, he thinks,
as he watches the first fiery showers bursting in the sky.
It is one of the most beautiful spectacles he's witnessed,
as if the sky was tearing open in bloom as
was his ventriculated heart.
The early cretaceous period was such bullshit.
It'll get better, just wait and you'll see.
In the meantime, we can hole up here in my cave,
we don't have to say anything,
just sit and wait out this asteroid storm.

In 2012 I sent an email to Justin Chin. It was just sort of a how are you doing, what's up kind of email. At the end I included a poem that I'd written entitled, "Faggot Dinosaur". My favorite thing about being a writer is being able to communicate with other writers in this way, an exchange of new work, and deep feelings and existential thoughts—even if you haven't been in touch for a while. Justin and I corresponded meaningfully, but infrequently. A while later he responded to my email and at the end said, "P.S. Did I ever show you my 'Faggot Dinosaur' poem inspired by your 'Faggot Dinosaur' poem?" I'd forgotten I'd ever even sent it to him.

After I read his poem I decided to collect submissions for artwork and poetry for a *Faggot Dinosaur* anthology. Within a month, I received over one hundred submissions from writers as far away as Moscow! If Justin had never responded to my poem with his poem I'd never had even done this project.

What I love so much about Justin's poem is that I can only see Justin in it as the dinosaur "on his haunches" in his cave. In the poem, the dinosaur takes every effort to make his painting, searching for the proper pigments. The dinosaur eats messily, thinks lewd thoughts, and then returns home to his cave to wait for "the world before them to evolve." The dinosaur in the poem didn't see the gravity of the asteroid coming toward the earth for what it was, but instead as "the sky tearing open in bloom."

The poem ends with the dinosaur couple planning to ride out the asteroid storm. In love, just watching and not saying anything. I think that's how most of us who knew Justin are trying to ride out his passing. I'm so grateful that the essence of him remains so vividly in his work.

Deal

Start with the dinosaur-shaped chicken nuggets,
the awfully cheap kind, mostly skin, feet
and tendons pulverized into a gristly chuck
that can only be good deep-fried in lard and eaten
in a diner laced with white bathroom tiles,
metal canteen tables and little children showing
their parents how animals copulate, all served
under the gaze of the big brown dog with a chef's hat dusty
from inviting the hungry, a stone's throw away
from the beach that lies across the highway (sea air's supposed to be
good for the soul), a much better class
of customer lies a spit away at the zoo.

Sad animals living in the wrong climate under
the watchful eyes of the paying public
who demand a show of all shows for their
bucks: eat something, scratch your pits,
play with those rubber toys, growl.
Watch the penguins stand with their wing-arms out,
relief from the heat in their Moses-themed pool
lined with reeds. The red-assed monkey clinging
to the wire cage pulling his butt hairs out.
The polar bear with fleas and skin allergies
gnawing on his arm. The Kodiak bear
about to die of heat stroke in his pen, which looks
not unlike the parking lot of a convenience store in Juneau.

Timing is everything. One false step to the salt-lick,
could have slept for three more hours
before going to the watering hole, and these animals
would still be free, not snagged and snared, hooked
and cargoed to this somber place. Timing could have sent them
to a better zoo, the ones where tropical rainforests
are created next to the savanna plains, so fur
and feather will remain gleaming, shiny,
groomed for all with admission tickets to see.

Other false move, and tiger's penis is served
in a bamboo steamer, bones brewed for aphrodisiac,
strength elixir, brand-name medicine sold
under counters while World Wildlife Fund monitors
shop for chinky souvenirs. One false move:
and bear's paw is stewed; antelope's horn is sawed;
elephant's tusk is carved into temple altar, paws
into wastebaskets, ears into fans; deer is delicious;
beaver is stuffed and put on mantle; kangaroo is dog food;
monkey is coconut-gathering friend; tiger is in magic show
in Vegas; baboon is heart transplant experiment;
orangutan is star of prime-time television sitcom;
rhino's horn is pickled; snake is broiled;
emu and ostrich taste like pork; iguana tastes like chicken;
chicken is skin and tendons, breaded in the shape of
ferocious Tyrannosaurus Rex, extinct, and his brutish
companion Brachiosaurus, extinct.

Start with a deliberate step, false even if you must.
Time it right, and irises bloom at night. Bergamot or bee
balm become the same medicine. Pomelos peel like grapes.
Forgiveness comes easy. Impatience and indecisiveness
as unsure as wild dreams. Cruelty and greed crumble
into heavy fools. Need is filled, gas station easy.
Tread in the tough language of a day, months,
a lifetime building up; anniversaries stacked babel-high.
If there is nothing but mere words, nothing
but time, I will squeeze my maudlin captive cravings
into a thousand cages filled with the beasts
of a million worlds. *Will you ever eat my heart?* Step
into the last empty cage, saved for us alone —

like fated animals and dinosaurs,
we are no more.

About the Writer

Justin Chin was born in Malaysia, raised and educated in Singapore, shipped to the U.S. by way of Hawaii, and resided in San Francisco for many years. He was the author of three books of poetry and one book of fiction, all published by Manic D Press: *Bite Hard* (1997); *Harmless Medicine* (2001), a Bay Area Book Reviewers Association Awards finalist; *Gutted* (2006), winner of the Publishing Triangle's Thom Gunn Award for Poetry; and *98 Wounds* (2011). Squeezed in between these were two non-fictions: *Mongrel: Essays, Diatribes & Pranks* (St. Martins, 1999) and the ur-memoir, *Burden of Ashes* (Alyson, 2002).

In the '90s, Chin also led a double life as a performance artist: he created and presented seven full-length solo works around the U.S. He packed up those cookies in 2002 (with occasional relapses) and the documents, scripts, and what-heck from that period were published in *Attack of the Man-Eating Lotus Blossoms* (Suspect Thoughts, 2005).

Chin taught at San Francisco State University, University of California at Santa Cruz, and Mills College. He garnered numerous grants and fellowships, including residencies at the Djerassi Foundation and Nebraska's KHN Center for the Arts. Among other awards, Chin receieved the *San Francisco Bay Guardian* Local Discovery Award in 1996 and apppeared on the newsweekly's cover. His work appeared in dozens of anthologies, literary journals, and magazines, ranging from *The Progressive* to *Drummer*. He twice represented San Francisco at the National Poetry Slam as a member of the San Francisco team, and performed his work throughout the US, including as part of the exhibit *Phantoms of Asia*, 2012, at the Asian Art Museum of San Francisco.

Justin Chin passed away in San Francisco, at the age of 46, from AIDS-related complications.

About the Book

All of the work in this collection has previously appeared in the following publications:

Bite Hard: pp 16, 18, 21, 23, 28, 35, 39, 42, 46, 47, 49, 52, 55, 67

Mongrel: pp 70, 140 (excerpt from "Q-Punk Grammar"), 160 (excerpt from "Slammed")

Harmless Medicine: pp 7, 24, 66, 83, 85, 87, 90, 91, 94, 97, 103, 113, 156

Burden of Ashes: pp 9, 141

Attack of the Man-Eating Lotus Blossoms: pp 26 (excerpt from "Born (1995-1998)"), 152 (excerpt from "These Nervous Days (1995-1999)")

Gutted: pp 25, 54, 89, 115, 116, 120, 123, 124, 126, 127, 128, 134, 135, 137

98 Wounds: 138

Faggot Dinosaur: 153

The editor gratefully acknowledges the talented writers and colleagues who contributed commentaries and personal reflections to this project: R. Zamora Linmark, Timothy Liu, Henry Machtay, Daniel Handler, Beth Lisick, Morgan Blair, Rabih Alameddine, Kevin Killian, Ali Liebegott.

…When you put a work out there, something happens to it. It is no longer the writer scrawling in his or her journal in some smoky café with a latte in hand, or writing in the solitude of an insomniac night. When you publish a piece of writing or perform it publicly, you give up a certain part of it, you do not own its meaning or its emotional control anymore. You want it to find an audience, and that audience will find its own meaning from reading or hearing that work. How they read and understand the piece will depend on so many things that are outside of the writer's control. Some people will look at the work on a purely emotional level and others on a more technical level, and still others will bring their whole life in literature to the table. But that's what the beauty of putting work out there is about.